D0952070

# The
# Hidden
# Agenda

Colombia para Cristo video introduction

Martin, that mountain is a mess.

Watch the *La Montaña* trailer, a film based on a true Stendal event

# The
# *Hidden*
# *Agenda*

An Extraordinary True Story Behind
Colombia's Peace Negotiations with the FARC

Russell M. Stendal
& Alethia Stendal

 ANEKO Press

Visit Russell's website: www.cpcsociety.ca

*The Hidden Agenda* – Russell M. Stendal

Copyright © 2014

First edition published 2014

Scripture taken from the Jubilee Bible®. Copyright © 2000 by LIFE SENTENCE Publishing. Used by permission. All rights reserved.

*Cover: Dugan Design Group*

*Cover and Vignette Images: nazlisart/Shutterstock*

*Editors: Sheila Wilkinson & Michelle Rayburn*

Printed in the United States of America

www.lifesentencepublishing.com

LIFE SENTENCE Publishing books are available at discounted prices for ministries and other outreach.

Find out more by contacting us at info@lspbooks.com

LIFE SENTENCE Publishing and its logo are trademarks of

LIFE SENTENCE Publishing, LLC

P.O. Box 652

Abbotsford, WI 54405

**POLITICAL SCIENCE / World / Caribbean & Latin American**

Paperback ISBN: 978-1-62245-184-5

Ebook ISBN: 978-1-62245-185-2

10  9  8  7  6  5  4  3  2

This book is available from www.amazon.com, Barnes & Noble, and your local bookstore.

Share this book on Facebook:

# Contents

Spring 2006 to Present.................................................................VII

**Part I** ........................................................................ XVII

    **Ch. #1:** Major Cordova ................................................. 1

    **Ch. #2:** Ever ..................................................................7

    **Ch. #3:** The Volcano ...................................................17

    **Ch. #4:** Sumapaz .........................................................25

    **Ch. #5:** Missionary Aviation....................................33

    **Ch. #6:** Steve ................................................................37

    **Ch. #7:** Eduardo Robayo and Jon Dufendach............47

    **Ch. #8:** Walter and Carrillo .................................55

    **Ch. #9:** The Least Shall Be the Greatest .....................63

    **Ch. #10:** When God Likes Something, He Multiplies It............73

**Part II**....................................................................... **83**

    **Ch. #11:** Eyes Shut Tight................................................85

    **Ch. #12:** Noel's Invitation .................................93

    **Ch. #13:** General Barrero....................................95

    **Ch. #14:** Fransisco Vergara's Kidnapping .....................97

    **Ch. #15:** God and the Colombians Will Know How to Thank You 99

    **Ch. #16:** The Private Meeting....................................103

    **Ch. #17:** The Island....................................................105

    **Ch. #18:** The Grace to Love Them ..............................109

    **Ch. #19:** Meeting Ivan.................................................111

    **Ch. #20:** The "Fetus"....................................................117

    **Ch. #21:** Freddy............................................................121

    **Ch. #22:** My Favorite Uncle.......................................125

    **Ch. #23:** Noel Meets Lisa and Sammy .........................127

    **Ch. #24:** Tom Howes ..................................................131

    **Ch. #25:** Trouble at Disney World..............................139

    **Ch. #26:** Hugo Tovar ..................................................147

    **Ch. #27:** President Uribe..............................................155

    **Ch. #28:** Uncle Clayt....................................................165

    **Ch. #29:** Clayt Sonmore in Cuba ...............................173

**Ch. #30:** The Voice of God............................................................181
**Ch. #31:** Forgiveness..................................................................189
**Ch. #32:** Albert Returns.............................................................193
**Ch. #33:** Jorge the Pirate ..........................................................197
**Ch. #34:** General Barrero...........................................................205
**Ch. #35:** The National Anthem...................................................215
**Afterword** ..................................................................................217
**Appx. #1:** Sin vs. Liberty...........................................................221
**Appx. #2:** Healings in Colombia................................................239

# Spring 2006 to Present

The agreement reached between the left-wing guerrillas of the 26th Front of the Armed Revolutionary Forces of Colombia (FARC) and the right-wing Centauros Block of the United Auto-Defense of Colombia (AUC) in the municipality of Cubarral, Meta, had both immediate and long term repercussions.

Both sides stopped killing civilians and backed off from the huge mountain over which they had been fighting, leaving it in my hands. I began to painstakingly de-mine the summit and the route where my engineers were cautiously installing steel towers to support high-tension electric lines so our large radio transmitter could be installed.

The campesino farmers, including many evangelical Christians who had been displaced from the area by all of the violence, began to return to their overgrown farms and deserted villages. In many cases, new trails had to be forged up the steep slopes because it was impossible to clear the mines off the old trails. We helped almost 600 children in one of the schools at the base of the mountain near the junction of the Tonoa and Ariari rivers. About 400 were orphans being raised by relatives because their parents had been killed up on the mountain.

This story is related in *Rescue the Captors 2* and in the full feature movie *La Montana*, produced and directed by my daughters, Lisa and Alethia.

In early 2006, the AUC Bloque Centauros paramilitary unit, led by Jorge Pirata (Jorge the Pirate) and Cuchillo (Knife), decided to surrender en masse to the Colombian government after being promised special conditions (which were later reneged on by the courts, causing the guerrillas to refuse to surrender since the promises of the government to the AUC were not kept). My brother, Chaddy, and I were asked to get up at 4:00 a.m. and drive two hours to the town of Casibare from our Lomalinda radio station in the municipality of Puerto Lleras. Casibare had been known as the capital of the paramilitary movement in our area.

We crept into the town just as dawn was breaking. Special Forces units of the Colombian Army and National Police had multiple rings of security around the entire area with orders to let anyone in, but no one out. As we pulled our old Toyota to a stop in front of the Casibare general store, all of a sudden both back doors of our vehicle were opened simultaneously, and top AUC commanders Cuchillo and Jorge Pirata both jumped into the back seat. It turned out they were concerned there could be a last-minute misunderstanding, even shooting, and wanted us to guarantee their surrender to the Colombian government, which took place a few minutes later.

General Saveedra, commander of the 7th Brigade, had been transferred to the Special Forces Rapid Deployment Brigade (FUDRA) and replaced by General Ardila, who supervised the surrender of the paramilitary forces. Colonel Leonardo Barrero, who had been chief of staff of the 7th Brigade, was transferred to Yopal, Casanare, and given the command of the 16th Brigade. Lt. Colonel Robinson, who had commanded the Alban Engineering Batallion with headquarters at Lomalinda, was also promoted. Many of the men and officers who had been stationed within range of our radio stations were strengthened and encouraged in their personal relationship with God as a result of our broadcasts and follow-up literature. This was the beginning of many deep and ongoing friendships, as over time men and officers from the 7th Brigade were transferred all over the country and new personnel were exposed to our ministry. It was not long before officers from all over began calling us and asking for our literature, Bibles, and Galcom radios to pass out to their men.

The same thing happened with the guerrillas. Soon I got word from Noel, who had also been promoted. We continued our relationship, which was always fraught with danger. Noel seemed to understand more and more of our message (he had all the books I had given him on a special shelf over his bed in the midst of his guerrilla camp). One day, I borrowed his transistor multi-band radio, which had five preset buttons, four of which were tuned to our stations. (We now had stations on FM, AM, and Shortwave). He asked me, in amazement, "How can you produce so many radio messages? How do you find time?"

I learned that a true sign of conversion is when these desperate men and women begin to demonstrate a genuine *hunger and thirst for righteousness* (Matthew 5:6). When a fierce terrorist commander starts listening to almost eight hours of Christian teaching and preaching a day over the radio, accompanied by intense study of the Bible and Christian literature, something is profoundly changing in their innermost being. The trials and testing of their faith will come in life or death real-life situations as they respond from a transformed heart. How different from many of those who raise their hand when every head is bowed and every eye is closed and then repeat a sinner's prayer after the pastor. How different from those who continue to attend endless church services and functions out of a guilt complex fostered by religiosity that does not offer victory. How different from those who primarily hear from their pastor or leader instead of coming under the direct discipline and authority of the Lord.

On the Communist station, *La Voz de la Resistencia*, every program was carefully scripted, and one hour of radio production often involved days of work for many people. Noel found it hard to understand how I could produce hundreds of hours of very hard-hitting programs in such a short amount of time. I explained that our programs simply flow as God moves in our hearts and this does not require scripting and a teleprompter. When we are in tune with the Spirit of God, we are tapped into an unlimited supply of wisdom and understanding from Him.

We would meet for hours and even days at a time and reflect on how to end the war in Colombia. This could only happen as hearts on all sides of the conflict are transformed by the power of God. Instead of drawing a line of conflict based on ideology, terrain, money, politics, religion, or so many other factors that influence war, we decided to draw a different line: those who are corrupt versus those who have clean hearts (and we made an exception to also include those who desire to have clean hearts even if this was not a reality quite yet).

So, Noel began to analyze those among his comrades and acquaintances who might fit this bill, and I began to do the same with the other sides. We began to target these people with our books, Bibles, and solar-powered radios locked on to our ministry frequencies. Many times we had members of opposite sides on the phone with each other, sometimes in tears.

At this time, one of the pastors who had a daily radio program on our Lomalinda FM station had been shot and killed by the guerrillas of the 27th Front along with his two sons. All eight evangelical churches in the nearby town of Puerto Lleras had been closed by order of a guerrilla commander nicknamed The Smurf, who had three brothers equally inclined. By a series of miracles, our stations were allowed to continue, but we had to produce all of our own programming because none of the local pastors dared to speak out.

After a close look – with legal counsel – at the US Patriot Act and other similar Colombian legislation, we began to take special precautions to avoid legal trouble with the governments of the United States and Colombia. It was very difficult for me to convince anyone in either government that there might actually be a few people in a designated terrorist group that might have good intentions – even in the midst of such a horrible war – and that we should cultivate people like this in a search for an end to the war.

Yet, slowly but surely, we began to acquire friends on all the different sides of the conflict who agreed that the real problem we were fighting begins with corruption deep inside the human heart, and unless this corruption is dealt with, conflict and war will only intensify. Somehow, as the years went by, I have always – by the grace of God – been able to have a legal covering, under which I have been able to operate with at least tacit approval from most of the powers that be. On many occasions, I have been on very thin ice, as verbal approval can quickly evaporate if everything hits the fan.

Many times, one guiding principle may have been the deciding factor preventing certain elements in government from prosecuting me. You see, I have always made it clear to everyone concerned that as we follow the scriptural advice to *overcome evil with good* (Romans 12:21), we will never do this in such a way as to aid and abet anyone who is still engaged in promoting evil. However, the strategy preferred by our real enemy, the Devil, is to pile on false accusations and slander from which only God can truly defend us. So if we are in the will of God, it is not wise to be overly concerned with defending ourselves.

On several occasions Noel and others were severely sanctioned by their own organization for following the dictates of their conscience. I soon realized we were all navigating a dangerous spiritual, moral, and even legal minefield.

Noel and I began to analyze the religious environment in Colombia. Left-wing elements in the Roman Catholic Church amalgamated a somewhat better relationship between some elements of the guerrillas and some elements of the church than the prevailing situation regarding Protestant Evangelicals. Even so, many Catholics have also been killed in this conflict, along with large numbers of evangelicals, including hundreds of pastors at the hands of the guerrillas and sometimes the mafias and paramilitaries. This has always been troubling to me, and I could see that Noel was also profoundly concerned. Most of the armed groups also tend on occasion to operate as proxies for seemingly upright people and entities that desire to remain incognito.

Noel and I had very good reason to suspect that radical – even atheist Marxist – priests were encouraging guerrilla leaders to persecute evangelicals. And there were extreme leftist pastors with no scruples trying to use the guerrillas to take out any religious competition. Noel had to keep fending off these kinds of attacks against me in the midst of all the other dangers. On top of this, we also have extreme right-wing religious leaders aligned with paramilitary remnants – and even with the mafia – that appear to have absolutely no scruples. This is reportedly the case with pastors of some of the largest churches in this country that are dedicated to a prosperity gospel that bypasses repentance and the cross.

Intense persecution, however, tends to draw all true believers together and weeds out religious persons whose hearts are corrupt and who are not sincere.

The roots of the guerrilla movement are a deep reaction against real and perceived corruption in both the economic and political realms, which prompts them to seek economic and political solutions, even to the point where they now contemplate being assimilated into democracy as they negotiate a peace treaty with the Colombian government.

However, I pointed out that there is a third realm, which is perhaps even more important than economics or politics. This is the religious realm. Real and/or perceived corruption in the religious realm has caused many guerrillas to throw the concept of God completely out the window. In this realm, they do not propose much of a solution, other than using left-wing pastors and priests as useful idiots to help them recruit marginal Christians and turn them into atheistic communists. When their position is taken to an extreme, we get North Korean-style communism being implemented in the mountains and jungles of Colombia by extreme force in which any mention or memory of God is carefully eradicated from all aspects of society.

The constant stream of incidents, such as priests abusing little boys and pastors fleecing entire congregations (along with the religious power plays mentioned above), sets the stage for the guerrillas to prohibit any expression of Christianity.

I began to search my heart before the Lord seeking a strategy that would not only work in rural areas of Colombia, where all religious meetings and activities have been banned by the Communists (in some areas for over sixty years), but for something that could be a beacon, an example, and a witness all over the world. It is under extreme adversity that true followers of Jesus Christ have always excelled. Some, like Richard Wurmbrand, spent long periods of time in solitary confinement and came out much stronger in the Lord. My own times in captivity and in prison have greatly strengthened my faith.

So, I decided: Let's not keep pretending that Christian meetings, rites, and rituals are essential under all circumstances. We will focus our ministry on individuals as Jesus did. When He sent out His disciples, He said that anyone who received one of His disciples received him, and if they receive Him, they also receive the Father who sent Him (Matthew 10:41). I became a sheep among wolves and repeatedly traveled through difficult areas restricted to pastors and missionaries to find out who would receive me as I came in the Name of the Lord. I never knew if each trip would be my last, or if I would ever return to my friends and family. Follow-up would be done over the radio and with parachute drops of Bibles, books, and Galcom radios.

As new Christians emerge, pure in heart, God joins them to one another – after they are clean – and dynamic leadership develops. The success has now surpassed even my wildest dreams as God takes the former misfits, persecutors, and troublemakers and turns them into modern-day editions of the apostle Paul.

We dropped the religious fluff and sanctimonious vocabulary. When your life is at stake for every idle word, it is best to speak only under the prompting of the Holy Spirit. I decided I would not volunteer information to those who were not asking the right questions unless specifically led to do so. This seems to fit exactly to the pattern Jesus used, and the results have been phenomenal. Now, many are following my example, joining individuals directly to Christ. This puts us on a track for a head-on collision with all the modern day scribes, Pharisees, and Sadducees dedicated to maintaining corrupt religious order by inserting themselves between the people and God.

There is a flurry of well-meaning and never-ending religious activity going on today that has actually caused generations of young people to quit attending church. Smothered with a carefully-planned religious program and agenda, many young people can't wait until they have enough autonomy to find the exits. Many church leaders are deluded into thinking they are following God when they are really yielding to a false religious spirit as Satan and his demons present themselves as angels of light (2 Thessalonians 2:11-12).

When repeatedly asked by guerrillas what I think of their movement, and at the same time knowing that they have virtually zero tolerance for criticism or dissent, I always respond, "You only lack one essential thing."

What is that? They always want to know. The answer, of course is they must first put God in His proper place. Then under His direction, everything else will be resolved.

What follows is a series of true stories that helped contribute to very intense spiritual awakening in Colombia. The lessons learned may have a wide application as persecution of Christians is increasing all over the world on a geometric progression. Not only in rural Colombia, but also all over the world in places like Egypt, Syria, Pakistan, Iran, China, Iraq, North Africa, and North Korea, it is now almost impossible to be a lukewarm Christian. What makes us think God will not allow lukewarm Christianity to be eradicated in North America?

As world events accelerate into the final days leading up to the return of our Lord Jesus Christ, it is not just the lukewarm who will be forced off of the fence to put their very lives on the line or to deny the Lord by their words and deeds. I firmly believe that all of man's seemingly good religious ideas are going to be found wanting. There is, however, a secure place of safety. It is my hope and prayer that the true testimonies in this book will be of edification and encouragement to many.

## Hebrews 12

*25 See that you do not refuse him that speaks. For if those who refused him that spoke on earth did not escape, much less shall we escape, if we turn away from him that speaks from the heavens,*

26 *whose voice then shook the earth; but now he has promised, saying, Yet even once, I shall shake not the earth only, but also the heaven.*

27 *And this word, Yet even once, signifies the removing of those things that are shaken, as of things that are made, that those things which cannot be shaken may remain.*

28 *Therefore, receiving a kingdom which cannot be moved, let us hold fast to the grace, by which we serve God, pleasing him with reverence and godly fear:*

29 *for our God is a consuming fire.*

Yes, man-made religion will crumble and fail in the face of the present and coming onslaught. Even seemingly good ideas and programs will not be able to stand if they tend to detract from and displace God's best.

For the Lord Jesus Christ will soon return for a bride without *spot or wrinkle or any such thing* (Ephesians 5:27).

Jesus said, *My sheep hear my voice, and I know them, and they follow me* (John 10:27), and will not follow the voice of another.

For those who are hearing the voice of the true shepherd, the coming difficult events will provide the greatest opportunity for harvest and victory that has ever been.

Please join us as we share testimonies of how God taught us to come with Him and *walk through the valley of the shadow of death and fear no evil* (Psalm 23:4).

Blessings,
Russell M. Stendal
November 29, 2013

# Part I

The Account Written
by Russell M. Stendal

# CHAPTER 1

# Major Cordova

Major Cordova, the Communications Officer for the 1st Brigade stationed in Tunja, the capital of the Department of Boyacá, was the epitome of bad behavior in the Colombia Army. Passed over for promotion on numerous occasions, his personnel file was full of black marks referring to insubordination, dereliction of duty, conduct unbefitting an officer, and so on.

I was under a lot of pressure trying to resolve a hostage situation involving Francisco Vergara in the so-called ABC triangle where the three Departments of Arauca, Boyacá, and Casanare met (one of the top hot spots in the country). Colonel Barrero, now commanding the 16th Brigade in Yopal, Casanare, had sent me up into the high mountains in one of his helicopters to install one of our radio transmitters in the hope we could influence the kidnappers in this very high-profile case. Alethia and I had been weathered in on top of a 12,800-foot mountain in extreme semi-arctic conditions for five days. The radio installation proved to be complex, and we were not looking forward to any more helicopter adventures.

I learned of a back road into the area from the Boyacá side, so I went to Tunja and spoke with Colonel Sergio Mantilla, the Brigade commander. He called in his B-2 intelligence officer who had an absolute fit at the idea of my attempting to reach the site by Toyota on the ground. In no uncertain terms, Army

Intelligence prohibited me from embarking on any adventures of this sort.

That is, until I got a surprise call from Major Cordova. He offered to go with me to the site, in spite of the outstanding orders against this, and we set up a midnight rendezvous at the central city square in Tunja. The major showed up in full combat uniform, complete with side arm and with his latest girlfriend in tow. We drove for hours back into the high Andes Mountains in an increasingly dense fog so thick it was hard to drive on the treacherous road. Somehow, we missed an important turn and meandered into guerrilla territory.

The guerrillas, however, were not to be seen. It so happened they were back where we had missed our turn, attacking the communications post that we were attempting to find. If we had driven into the middle of the firefight, I am certain that they would have either executed or captured the major. And who knows if the girl and I would have also been killed in the crossfire? We got so lost that we eventually had to find a campesino with an old jeep and have him guide us back to the right crossroads. We finally drove onto the base at about 8:30 a.m., about an hour after the guerrilla attack had ceased.

After three or four more trips that were never dull, we got our equipment running properly and helped resolve four separate hostage situations. When Colonel Mantilla found out about it, he authorized our radio broadcasts to continue, and God was able to touch many people in both Colombia and Venezuela through those broadcasts, which continue to this day. Within a few months, both Sergio Mantilla and Leonardo Barrero were promoted to the rank of general by President Uribe.

As a new general, Leonardo Barrero was given command of the 29th Brigade in Popayan in the Department of Cauca. One of his first deeds when he arrived was to call me and arrange for Christian FM radio coverage into his area to reach all the different factions, starting with the indigenous groups. Somehow Major Cordova got transferred over to Popayan, his hometown, as the new communications officer for Barrero. One day, I got an unexpected phone call from the general, raving about the transformation that had come over Cordova. He wanted to know what I had done to convert a hopeless, black sheep into such a competent, reliable, courteous, respectful, and even delightful Christian officer.

I was at a complete loss as to how to answer the general because I had never attempted to push the major into any type of religious conversion experience. He had not gone to any services that I knew of, and none of us had even attempted to lead him in a simple prayer of salvation. His conversion had come upon him like the dawning of a new day. He had been in total darkness, and now he was definitely walking in the light with a totally new set of appetites and demonstrating the fruit of the Holy Spirit. Instead of the key points of his pilgrimage being church meetings, altar calls, baptism, communion, repetitious prayers, Christian how-to seminars, or even Bible reading, the waypoints on his journey were when he risked his life to help me go on wild adventures to broadcast the gospel into one of the most depraved areas in the world. Many, many more cases like this were to follow.

## Colonel Cardona

The next commander of the 1st Brigade in Tunja was Colonel Cardona who had been the aide to General Reynaldo Castellanos (Evangelical Christian commander of the entire Colombian Army). I was introduced to Castellanos by retired General Gabriel Diaz who knew my father from when he was a 2nd lieutenant. Castellanos was aware of our literature and radio endeavors, which he heartily backed. However, his time as Army Commander soon came to a tragic end. There is a law on the books in Colombia requiring all Armed Forces officers to be Roman Catholic. This had been overlooked to some degree, as hundreds were becoming evangelical. But the general's wife was quite an activist. Soon she had revival meetings and late night prayer vigils – with reported mandatory attendance – going on at many of the key military bases. The general would have all his staff down on their knees for long prayer times before their staff and strategy meetings. Militarily, Reynaldo Castellanos was one of the most brilliant and successful generals in Colombian history, as he broke the guerrilla blockade that was strangling the capital city of Bogotá. I spoke with him on a Friday night, and he proudly told me about all the evangelical religious activities going on at the Army bases. He told me that God would protect him in his job as long as he continued to put God first, and he bubbled over with more plans to promote the participation of even more of the military personnel in these obviously sincere religious endeavors.

On Monday, disaster struck. The law about military officers being required to be Roman Catholics was reportedly applied without warning. General Castellanos was fired. He could not believe it. All of his Christian friends were stunned. Since Monday was a US holiday (President's Day) but not a Colombian holiday, not even his good friends at the US Embassy found out in time to help him. Soon other Christian officers resigned, were passed over for promotion, or were fired. The nemesis of Castellanos, General Mario Montoya, was now commander of the Colombian Army. I was crestfallen as well. This happened just a few days before a secret meeting was to take place between General Castellanos and some top guerrilla commanders who were contemplating God and peace. With Montoya in place, this meeting was completely out of the question.

I got a call from Colonel Cardona in Tunja, and he wanted us to distribute Galcom radios, Bibles, and as much literature as possible to more than 8000 of his men. Boyacá is noted for having some of the best soldiers, and this is also where the key battles for Colombian independence from the Spaniards were fought. We had almost finished distributing our materials to the 1st Brigade when angry superiors ordered Colonel Cardona to desist. Within a few months, he was passed over for promotion to general and forced to leave the Colombian Army even though his career was brilliant. Many of the soldiers with our materials were later transferred into units all over Colombia, spreading revival.

Christian officers soon learned not to wear their Christianity on their sleeves. They had to learn the same lessons that Noel and I were learning and applying in the guerrilla areas. God began making it very clear that he was not calling us to religious hype and meetings, particularly if there were any guilt trips or any form of coercion associated with Christian activity. No, we were being called to simply walk with the Lord 24/7.

I had been preaching before live audiences in a community center in Bogotá with the purpose of recording and broadcasting these messages over the radio into areas of extreme unrest. The messages were timeless and could be used over and over. The series on Daniel was transcribed by Alethia and edited into a great book by my son-in-law, Sammy. The approach Daniel took when he was captured and then rose to great prominence in pagan kingdoms held many key lessons for us. Colonel Cardona gave one of my Daniel books to Luis Humberto Montejo, ex-governor of Boyacá. Luis Humberto read the book twice from cover to cover and then got Cardona to invite me over for dinner so he could meet me face to face.

It turned out that Luis Humberto had gone through an experience very similar to that of General Castellanos. When he became governor, he had attempted great reforms as an Evangelical Christian. He happily fired hundreds of corrupt state employees and canceled the contracts of corrupt business people (most of whom were Roman Catholics) and gleefully continued grand reformation on about the same scale as King Josiah in the Bible until he came to almost the same fate. The swift reaction to his noble efforts completely blind-sided him, and Luis Humberto was forced out of power after only four months in office. Over 1000 irate people, whose very existence had been threatened, all filed lawsuits against him. Luis Humberto was still licking his wounds when the Daniel book was placed in his hands, and we became instant friends. His beautiful wife, Elsa, was in quite a depression over all of what had happened to them. She requested all of our radio messages and sat in her spectacular home that she had designed, which overlooked Tunja, and listened to hundreds of messages until her depression left and never came back.

# CHAPTER 2

# Ever

I continued the messages on weekends at the community center named Los Heroes in Bogotá. I would count until the first twenty people showed up and then launch a message, preaching through the Bible one chapter per message. By the time I finished the first message, the meeting room would be full. Then we would sing for a few minutes, and I would give the second message. This helped build up our stock of radio programs.

One day, a short fellow with penetrating eyes walked up to speak with me after a message. Ever was from Muzo, the emerald mining district in Boyacá. He was definitely touched by the Lord, and since I have had the emerald miners on my heart for a long time, I invited Ever to come home with me. Then, since he had a vehicle, I loaded him up with about twenty boxes of Bibles and Galcom radios to distribute to the miners.

It was quite a while afterwards that I found out who Ever really was. The big mines have enforcers known as *pajaros* (birds). These men kill whomever the *patron* (or owner) tells them to kill. The mines are in constant warfare. Ever was a pajaro who was in charge of other pajaros. He had been killing people since he was a teenager.

Things had not been going well for him, and he felt it was his fault that several of his family members had been killed.

Enemies were on his tail trying to kill him too. His mother, sister, and wife were all Christians and somehow had brought him to our meeting.

He went out to a farm with the materials I had given him and started listening to us on the radio. This caused him to become interested in the Bible. After forty days, he went back to Muzo and began to preach and share a testimony to the town about how filthy and despicable he had been and how God had cleaned up his heart. He asked the entire town to forgive him. Even his enemies who were trying to kill him forgave him and now their families have also come to the Lord.

As Ever continued to listen to us on the radio, he had some nagging doubts about whether or not we were for real. He had seen a lot of religious hypocrisy. So he came out to see our Lomalinda radio station for a week with his mother, his sister, and his wife. They were concerned for me, and each one took turns taking me aside and telling me about all the awful things Ever had done. They said we could not be sure that he was really converted, and they were afraid he could still get mad at someone and kill them, as this had been the pattern of his life.

At Lomalinda, our radio personnel had been accustomed to having all of their meals together in a common dining room for fellowship and to make the radio ministry more efficient. After much infighting and backbiting took place between our people, my wife and I and our station manager decided to suspend the group meals and have every family cook their own food to try to get things back on an even keel. Hopefully, we could try again in the future, and folks would be more appreciative of one another and of the meals.

One day, I felt a strong urge to start up the communal kitchen and dining room again. My wife and Elsa, our station manager, disapproved because there was still some bickering going on among some of our staff – but I overrode them and ordered the group meals to start immediately.

The first meal was Monday breakfast, and this is when Ever and his relatives unexpectedly showed up at the radio station to see if we were for real. He left a week later saying that he had never seen such wonderful, loving, kind, Christian people like us before in his life.

So now, Ever wanted to organize a large evangelistic meeting to reach Muzo, the emerald capital of Colombia, with the gospel. And he wanted me to be the main speaker. I knew enough about Muzo from sporadic previous events to know that this was not going to be easy, but I felt impressed in my spirit to say yes.

The main religion for much of Colombia is not really Roman Catholicism. It is a brand of spiritism, which includes worship of the dead and communication with spirits in the underworld that allegedly control physical safety, financial prosperity, and other favors. Each of the major emerald magnates had their *brujo*, or spiritist. They only felt secure if their brujo was better than the brujos of their enemies.

According to Ever, the demands from the spirit world had degenerated into a horrible litany of killings directed by the brujos and carried out by the pajaros. The key mine owners would meet with their brujos in tow and place an enameled plate on the table surrounded by photos of all of their worst enemies. In the plate they would place the index finger (preserved in formaldehyde) of the last person they had killed, and at the appropriate moment in their spiritist rites, they would spin the finger in the plate. When the finger came to rest, whoever's picture at which it pointed would become the next victim the pajaros were supposed to kill (and then put the new finger in the formaldehyde).

The most powerful brujo on record was a man named Jesús

Saria, whose wife, known in Colombia as the Monita Retrechera, had been murdered in a scandal that allegedly touched the presidential level. Jesús had been sent to prison in an effort to get him out of the way and prevent him from causing any more trouble. However, in prison he had an encounter with God. Aided by a Christian prison warden, Jesús Saria took a prison correspondence course and was ordained as a minister. After a few years, he was released from prison and went back to Muzo. Jimmy Molina, heir to one of the big mines, hired Saria because in one of the satanic spiritist rites, the finger had reportedly pointed at his picture. He was running scared and wanted the most powerful brujo he could find.

Jesús Saria told Jimmy Molina what had happened to him in prison and that now everyone must follow the Lord. However, Saria had become like the blind man touched by Jesus who saw men walking as trees and needed another touch from the Master. Saria managed to displace most of the brujos in Muzo, but he replaced them with prosperity gospel pastors who told the mine owners that their safety, security, and prosperity now depended on the mine owner paying tithe money from their emerald mines to the pastors. Saria was happily walking through the mines pronouncing blessings and giving big prophecies about where to find rich veins of emeralds in exchange for the tithe money. Jimmy even made him a partner, and I heard that they actually found a lot of emeralds.

However, now they had all become concerned about all the local unconverted "sinners" in Muzo, which was little more than a haphazard collection of bars and brothels and worse. The town square, unlike most in Colombia, had been roofed over and made into a giant arena that could seat thousands. This was surrounded on at least three sides with wall-to-wall bars and houses of ill repute. The plan was to get a high-powered sound system capable of booming through the entire town and bring in a high-powered evangelist (me) so that all the poor drunks and prostitutes could be saved.

They proceeded to commandeer the "worship" band from a local Unitarian Church which had all kinds of instruments to bang and clang – but not too much in the line of melody – and invited the Christians from all the local churches along with all the pastors. This was the situation into which we walked.

My son-in-law, Sammy, started to get cold feet the night before when we were all sleeping in a mine bunkhouse with an exuberant Jesús Saria, who exclaimed that this was perfect timing because it was a full moon.

"Full moon?" asked Sammy, puzzled.

"Yes," came the reply, "this is when all the spirits are most active, and so I invite you all to join me at midnight under the full moon as I invoke the Holy Spirit on our meeting tomorrow." Saria cheerfully rambled on as Sammy eyed the door. At some point, I drifted off to sleep exhausted from the long drive over difficult roads.

They had made a high platform at one end of the arena, and the band was in full swing by the time we got there. I had never heard such awful noise. Right in front of the immense platform were three or four rows of about fifty seats each – with ample space in front and back – reserved for pastors. Thousands of seats were filling up rapidly with townspeople and others who came from miles around who either were Christians or had some affinity for the meeting. Sammy sat beside me at the end of one of the rows reserved for the pastors, holding his head in his hands as it was impossible to even think above the din.

Dozens of prosperity pastors had come in from Bogotá complementing their local counterparts, and every seat in the ministry section was full. They wanted to be like Jesús Saria and help all the miners and mine owners prosper in exchange for all that tithe money. Jimmy Molina and several others close to the status of billionaires were coming in with their carloads of bodyguards to sit in special seating prepared for them. Sammy got up and went outside for a minute to catch his breath, and immediately a lady pastor who was waiting breathlessly for the event to commence took Sammy's seat.

When Sammy came in and saw that his seat was taken, he told me that this was such a hopeless mess that there was nothing we could do here in such an impossible situation. Sammy said he was leaving and invited me to go with him.

I said, "No, the Lord just showed me what to do. When I get up to speak, you sit in my place and pray."

Jesús Saria told about our family coming to Colombia in 1964 and said that I was one of the most qualified missionary/ evangelists in the country. He gave me a grand introduction and went on and on and told all the pastors and people how wonderful the meeting was going to be. Then it was my turn.

The Lord had told me to preach, not to the town, but to the rows of preachers sitting right in front of my nose at point blank range. I used some of the events described in *Rescue the Captors 2* as illustrations because many of the paramilitary leaders got their start in Muzo and some even continued to work for the emerald bosses. Hearing the accounts of what God had done in the lives of some of their own even started to draw people out of the bars and cat houses. They pressed their noses up against the windows running all around the huge central arena.

When everyone was spellbound, at the prompting of the Holy Spirit, I lowered the boom. I asked them if they would like to see the town of Muzo converted to Jesus Christ and cleaned up. All the religious people in the audience cheered. Then I looked square at the lines of chairs right in front of the podium containing close to 200 preachers and spoke. "How can we have a genuine, lasting revival here in this town if we have corruption and wrong desires in the hearts of the ministers of the gospel? Who are we to think that we own money that belongs to God? As ministers, are you willing to turn your backs on the things of this world so that you can truly be effective in the community? Are you willing to make a public commitment before God and before this town that you are willing to be disciplined and dealt with by God as he sees fit in order for your motives in ministry to be pure?"

Now people started pouring out of the cantinas and houses of ill repute. People were coming from all over town to see what was going to take place with all those pastors. Word went through the bars, "Some American is laying into all those obnoxious pastors who have been after our money!" It was wild.

I started pacing up and down the long 100-foot platform, keeping myself at point blank range of all those prosperity preachers. Finally, I said, "The time has come to make a public covenant of trust between you who are in the ministry and God. This needs to be witnessed by the people of this town. If you are in agreement with all that I have said and truly desire to be accountable to God and to the people, I invite you ministers to stand to your feet. We are going to present ourselves as living sacrifices before the throne of God."

There was deathly silence. Only two pastors stood up. Their knees were trembling. A third joined them – I think it was Sammy. Then attention shifted to the back of the huge crowd. During the meeting, someone had wheeled in a paralyzed lady, around fifty years old, who was well known in town and who had spent a very long time in the wheelchair. All of a sudden, the paralyzed lady stood up and began to walk! She said afterwards that when she heard me say, "Stand up if you want to make a total commitment and be accountable to God," she immediately knew that she would be able to make the commitment, and so she did. When that happened the entire multitude rose to its feet.

When the crowd stood up, the pastors all started looking at one another and standing up too. The paralyzed lady made it to the front of the auditorium, pushing her wheelchair. I gave the microphone back to Jesús Saria. Sammy and the rest of our crew began distributing our truckload of Bibles to the crowd. They distributed a copy of my book on Daniel to all the preachers. The worship team came back, and instead of banging and clanging they broke forth into a deep, sweet, anointed melody.

In tears, Jesús Saria said that he needed another touch from God. That he was placing his heart on the altar. That God could deal with him however God saw fit. He went on and on.

Jimmy Molina took Sammy and me along with Ever down into his mine. He found a huge green emerald about half the size of my fist and gave it to me. It was huge but turned out to be fairly low quality. I gave it to Voice of the Martyrs (VOM) to put in their museum in Bartlesville. Ever showed us how the Galcom shortwave radios work deep inside the mines, thousands of feet underground. The electric lines plumbed through the tunnels serve as giant antennas, and the radios work perfectly. Many miners continue to listen to us on the radio.

Our heart went out to Jimmy Molina and to his beautiful wife. He was touched by us and by the message, but like the rich young ruler in the gospel, he found it impossible to make a total commitment. Later, Jesús Saria had another dose of legal trouble and was put back into prison. We are praying that the Lord will touch him again and give him 20/20 spiritual vision this time. After Saria went back to prison, Jimmy Molina became the pastor of his own prosperity church.

Ever began to preach and has had a dynamic ministry for the past eight years since his conversion. It began on a Sunday morning when he walked into one of the largest prosperity churches in Tunja. With one hand behind his back, Ever walked onto the platform in the middle of the Sunday morning service and demanded the microphone. Most of the people knew his background and were terrified. They thought he had a gun or a hand grenade. Fifteen minutes into his message, the amazed audience saw Ever bring his hand out from behind his back. He was holding one of our green Galcom radios.

At the end of the message, the senior pastor repented and ended up resigning from the denomination. Today Miguel Contreras lives by faith as a missionary in the Catatumbo area of the Colombia-Venezuela border ministering to guerrillas, soldiers, paramilitary, and corrupt government personnel on both sides of the border.

# CHAPTER 3

# The Volcano

B ack at Lomalinda, a storm was brewing over the horizon. A Catholic bishop in a major town within range of one of our stations perceived a huge problem. Most of the ladies who had faithfully attended his early morning mass for years failed to show up repeatedly. He did some quick detective work and discovered they were meeting for prayer and fellowship at the home of one of the ladies. So, he interrupted their next meeting and told them it was illegal for them to have a Catholic meeting without Roman clergy being present and in charge. He was cordially but firmly informed that this meeting was not under the Church. They were meeting under the auspices and covering of Russ's radio station, unbeknownst to me.

The bishop also had a radio station. His radio journalist, who for some reason had a chip on his shoulder, wrote a letter of complaint addressed to the president and called for the closure of our stations. Without further ado, the bishop signed the letter, which was sent to the Presidential Palace with a cooperative senator of the Republic. Down at the palace, the letter was not given directly to the president; it was sent over to the lady Minister of Communications who was a strong member of the Catholic Opus Dei, a semisecret Catholic society focused on political power that reports directly to the Papal Nuncio and to the Vatican.

I was with Alethia on a trip back into the mountains to see Noel. After spending a few days with him, we went farther back into guerrilla territory and found Giovani. His men were "chewing on" some of our materials. One of them, Antonio Campesinos, had a terrible reputation but always seemed to like me. Maybe it was because I got him some reading glasses so he could read our books. He even seemed excited when I gave him a Bible. On the way, Alethia shot a picture of me giving Galcom radios to some guerrillas of the 40th Front. A control officer almost took away the camera. The picture made the cover of the VOM magazine.

Giovani helped us take VOM action packs and give them to all the children in his area. The beautiful backpacks were in the colors of the Colombian flag and had the VOM logo. Every child received a radio, a Bible, and a nice toy among many other items. Who would have ever thought that such a tough guerrilla commander would have such a heart for children? He had been responsible for some of the greatest defeats in the history of the Colombian military. One of my guys offered to give Giovani his watch if Giovani would thoroughly read my Daniel book. Arrangements were made to come back later and quiz Giovani on the book to see if he had really read it.

When we got back into the realm of civilization, several major things had happened. There were over sixty missed calls on my phone as Marina had been frantically trying to find Alethia, who had not clued her mother in as to where we were going, as I had thought she had. Marina was so relieved, she was not able to get very mad at us.

Back at Lomalinda, it was another story. A team of experts from the Ministry of Communications had come out and gone over all of our radio installations with a fine tooth comb, finding fourteen real or imagined discrepancies. We were being sued by the government on all points. Fortunately, a few weeks before, a friend had offered us prepaid legal services for $125 per month for each of our radio frequencies. They ended up doing tens of thousands of dollars of expert legal work for $125 a month.

As these serious legal processes made their way through the bureaucracy, they encountered secret admirers of ours embedded in the system who would make the paperwork disappear. So the legal counsel for the Ministry of Communications had to start over and painstakingly repeat the process. This happened several times and dragged things out for many months.

Finally our ten-year charter for the FM frequency ran out, and the Ministry stonewalled our application for renewal. It looked like we would lose our FM and possibly even our AM and Shortwave frequencies. By this time, we were almost finished with a Galcom project to distribute 100,000 solar-powered radios, fix-tuned to our frequencies, which could not be easily recalled or reprogrammed. Over three million dollars was invested. If we lost our legal battles, what would I say to the donors?

Our lawyer thought we would most likely lose but decided to make one last power play without my knowledge. Since he had power of attorney from us, he sued the Minister of Communications in our name with a *tutela,* or lawsuit, which gave her a two-week time period to either renew our license or prosecute us to the fullest extent of the law. She could not simply stay back and let our application time out.

This was no sooner accomplished (with me in the dark), and I was driving across the mountains when my cell phone rang. It was Major General Jairo Herrazo, Commander of the 5th Division, who said, "Pay attention; the president wants to speak with you!"

I wondered if he was pulling my leg because he always had quite a sense of humor, but I pulled over and paid attention. President Uribe – whom I had met back in 1980 when, as Civil Aeronautics Director, he had helped me with my pilot's license

– came on and told me he was facing an emergency and the general had told him I was the right person who could help. A volcano named Machin, rated as one of the most dangerous volcanoes in the world, had begun to erupt in the Municipality of Cajamarca. The president said he had been following my work and wished to congratulate me. He wanted to know if I could mount a radio station in a position to cover the entire disaster area and provide solar-powered radios to anyone living in a place of imminent danger. He wanted me to set up a good warning system for the people, and he told me I would also be free to share the gospel over the new station.

A few weeks before, David Witt of SOM had led a group of men from Arizona and visited us. Then they sent an offering for over fifty thousand dollars. When I asked them if it was designated for anything special, they said that it was for whatever the Holy Spirit prompted me to do with it. So the money was sitting there in the bank.

I told the president I would do it right away. He said that in two days he would fly to Ibague at the foot of the mountain with the Minister of Communications and meet me there. I continued to Lomalinda and loaded up all of our emergency equipment and antennas. Meanwhile, all of our staff focused on this project. It was amazing. Over a hundred people worked thirty-six hours straight. At the end we were on the air on a clear frequency in an area saturated with FM signals on top of a huge mountain overlooking the volcano. Since there was so little time to give formal orders or even unnecessary phone calls, most of our people had to simply be led by the Lord, and everything came together.

I went to the Ibague airport to meet the president after working almost forty-eight hours straight. General Herrazo was there having a press conference with international media. The governor and the mayor were holding forth when the Minister of

Communication and her staff came in. The president had been unable to make it and my heart sank. She took the microphone, answered a few questions, and then at the end of her remarks said, "And regarding this Evangelical radio station that has been mentioned, I will study the situation and give an answer of whether or not this is viable in six months."

General Herrazo took the microphone and said, "With all due respect, Madam Minister, we obey the orders of our Commander in Chief, President Uribe. He gave us the order, the radio station is now on the air, and what we need from you without any further delay is the permission."

I did not have to say a word in public.

The general then took the minister and ushered her together with me into the VIP inner sanctum where he introduced us. She took a good look at me, and her legal advisor, who had gone through all the trouble of trying to sue us over and over, tried to crack a thinly veiled joke with the general that was at least half serious. "General," he said, "you don't realize exactly who this American is. If you really knew about half of the stuff he has done, you would have him arrested and given life in prison!" Sitting across from me was another aide to the minister who secretly supported us and may have been the one who kept making the legal paperwork against us disappear. She cracked a grin.

The minister looked at me with a serious look and said, "Why did the president pick you? What makes you qualified to do this?"

I replied, "Ever since we helped solve the kidnapping of his friend, Francisco Vergara, the president has been extremely friendly to us." My daughters and my wife came forward and were introduced. They had stayed up all night making cookies for the president, which the minister promised to deliver.

We were all supposed to climb aboard a military Blackhawk

helicopter and survey the disaster area. The weather refused to cooperate. We were stuck in the small VIP room for three hours with the Minister of Communications, her staff, and General Herrazo. I explained all about Richard Wurmbrand and VOM and gave her copies of all of our books. I told her how Richard Wurmbrand had worked together with Roman Catholics to help bring down the Iron Curtain with Bibles, literature, and radio broadcasts – just as we were doing in Colombia. I told her that our purpose and campaign was to direct a message to individuals calling them to repentance and into a personal relationship with God with clean hearts so that the Holy Spirit could lead us all. Three hours later, when she got up to leave, she held out her hand to me and said, "You can count on that permission; you have my word."

A few days later, our lawyer got a letter from her lawyer calling off the Lomalinda lawsuits and informing us that the charters for our radio stations that had expired would be renewed for another ten years. Then a few days later, the permission came through for the new radio station named after the volcano, Machin Estereo.

General Herrazo became an excellent friend along with one of his key staff officers named Paco Mejia. Paco worked out all the details for the radio station and for many other great projects to propel our message and literature into difficult, hard to reach places.

I had a friend introduce me to the bishop out in the Llanos who had signed the initial letter against us and was able to make a friend out of him. He told me that someone else had written the letter and he should have never signed it without checking us out first.

The journalist who wrote the letter had come down with throat cancer and died a few months before I met with the bishop.

The senator who took the letter to the Palace was later

accused before the Supreme Court of unauthorized visits to the paramilitary, and as far as I know is still in jail.

On another occasion, I was invited by my friend, General Gabriel Diaz, to a military ceremony for the ascension of Mario Montoya to lieutenant general. I was given the honor of sitting in the special box with all the retired generals, right next to the reviewing stand. The Diplomatic Corps was four stands down at the very end. On his way out of the event, President Uribe walked right past the US Military delegation headed up by a two star US General from Southcom, went over to General Diaz who was a few feet from me and gave him a hearty greeting. Then he walked twenty-five feet or so to the door and disappeared. To my utter consternation, all of a sudden he came back in the door, walked up to me, shook my hand, and then walked back out the door right in front of everybody. I learned he had one of our Galcom radios on his desk that he was fond of listening to at night in the wee hours if he could not sleep.

# CHAPTER 4

# Sumapaz

The Colombian Armed Forces made a major push against the guerrilla forces stationed along the base of the eastern ridge of the Andes between Lejanias and La Uribe, Meta. Tens of thousands of soldiers fought hard against thousands of guerrillas. In just one day, it is rumored that more than fifty soldiers lost their feet by stepping on land mines. In the midst of this turmoil, it was reported that the guerrilla founder, Manuel Marulanda Velez, died from a heart attack in the arms of his sentimental companion.

Noel and many others that I knew were pushed up into the Sumapaz high country. I received a desperate phone call telling me how to find him. Sumapaz is noted for being a very closed society. Not even Roman Catholic churches are allowed. Many strangers who stray into Sumapaz disappear. It is known as the largest Alpine meadow in the world. All of the terrain above the 11,000-foot timberline is glaciated. The wide, U-shaped valleys descend into tight Vs at the magic 11,000-foot level. The peaks rise majestically to over 14,500 feet.

I took my brother, Chaddy, my electronics engineer, Abel, and my tower structure engineer, Luis. Luis had been up there months before, working on a radio tower someone had put on one of the mountains. We managed to find the remote school where we were told to rendezvous with our guide, a guerrilla also named Luis. The contact man named Hilber was a likable fellow who managed a local store. We finally made contact with the guide late in the day and were told it was a four-hour hike so we wanted to get going immediately. By the time a mule was provided for my 240-pound brother, it was past 3:00 p.m. As we hiked up into 13,000-foot territory, it was hard to move fast or make good time.

Night caught us on the upper *paramo*, and our guide told us that if we did not keep moving, we would all freeze to death in the bitter subfreezing temperature with a howling wind. All we had were the dim lights from our cell phones to guide us through an incredible maze of rabbit trails and old cow paths. At one point Chaddy generously offered me his mule. We were on the side of a cliff when it started to buck. In the shadow of our flashlights, it had seen a dead bush. Somehow I managed to get off the mule in one piece. Luis, the engineer, was smart. He had stayed behind with Hilber beside the road with our Toyota.

Abel was strong as an ox, but from the city and not used to this. His ankle began to give out, and he began to pull toward any downhill cow path. I had a lot of trouble keeping him going uphill without losing the others. Luis and I figured we had to keep Abel moving, even though he begged to rest. If he stopped, we feared his ankle would freeze up, and we would be stuck in an extremely dangerous situation. It would also be very easy for someone to wander a few hundred yards off track in the dark. The wind would drown out any call for help. The mist made our lights all but useless. After what seemed an eternity, we made it over the last rise and descended thousands of feet into a hidden valley that was a long-time hideout of top guerrilla commanders.

At about midnight, we arrived at a very snug cabin, complete with a flush toilet, wood paneled ceiling, and beds with lots of wool blankets. The next morning we walked through what seemed to be a magic wonderland of moss-covered trees in the midst of lush grass paddocks. The select local people made their living milking cows and making cheese, which was hauled out on pack mules.

The next farm belonged to a campesino nicknamed Bigfoot because his feet were so big he had to have special-order boots. Luis was trying to tell us that the guerrilla camp was another eight hours, but lo and behold Noel showed up at the house of Bigfoot, saving us seven hours of walking.

We all spent the next night at Bigfoot's place in a huge bunkroom with only one door and small windows. It was cold. At about four in the morning, one of the guerrillas tried to go outside to the bathroom. The door had a homemade latch with a big six-inch nail wound with a nylon rope like a Rube Goldberg masterpiece. Abel, who was the last one to come in for the night, had secured the door in such a way that no one could get it back open. Being a city boy, he was thinking about the possibility of cougars or jaguars or bears, all of which roam the area. But at 4:00 a.m., we had the sight of the guerrilla dancing around in a hurry to get to the bathroom but unable to open the door. Finally, he had to call Bigfoot who was able to cut the rope with his machete from the outside. As the guerrilla disappeared outside to take his leak, his last words were, "But who would do such a thing?" Chaddy and Abel and I lay there with our heads under our blankets, and nobody said a word.

This was the beginning of dozens of trips into this secluded guerrilla inner sanctum. We were able to haul VOM action packs (they had sent us a container with 10,000) to every kid for miles around. Luis, our guerrilla guide, helped us find all the schools and place the materials, even though each neighborhood communist syndicate looked at us with a lot of distrust. These were and are some of the most dangerous trips I have ever made due to the high altitude, the terrain, the weather, and the fact that in order to optimize time, this all needed to be done on horseback.

The rewards were astounding. Bigfoot and many of his neighbors became strong Christians. We were allowed to put a radio station on top of the highest mountain we could find, which was a real challenge. We dragged the light poles straight up the side with a remarkable team of oxen. We built cabins and bathrooms in strategic places. All the children loved us. They would take the solar Galcom radios and use them to evangelize their parents and even the guerillas if they came by for a night. After I had several accidents on horseback, breaking my ribs and my wrist, some of my guys got together and bought me a beautiful mountain horse that I christened Silver. I always sawed off the saddle horns on my saddles because several times the horse went down, and I stayed on but broke ribs against the saddle horn.

Once I took Marina up there, and our good riding horses were somewhere else, so we rode the pack horses. Hilber and his brother, Juan, had two dogs, Oso and Arracacho, which were at least half wolf. Not even their owners could pet them. I had made friends with the dogs on a previous trip when I brought an inflatable boat, which we tried out in a beautiful glacial lake teaming with trout. The lake had ice on it in the mornings that broke and piled up on the leeward side when the sun came out and the wind picked up. The dogs jumped into the water and tried to follow us. They soon got all cramped up and started to drown in the cold glacial water. Their owners, never having been in a boat before and unable to swim, did not relish the thought of trying to fish in the dogs even if the dogs did not try to bite them with their razor sharp teeth. I looked at Arracacho and it appeared to me that he genuinely wanted help. So I grabbed him and pulled him into the boat. Then I did the same with the second dog. After that, I was the only one the dogs would allow to pet them. If I ever came by and went on my horse out into the paramo, they would leave their owners and go with me.

On this trip, I had Marina on one packhorse led by Juan, and I was on the other with just a rope halter and no bit or bridle. This went okay until Oso and Arracacho came out of nowhere chasing a rabbit under the horse. With no bit, I was unable to keep my horse's head down, and the next minute I was airborne. I broke my left wrist and three ribs, one high in the back, one on the side, and one low in the front. But I did not realize it at the time. So after I got my wind back, I climbed back on the horse, which seemed to be the best way to get back out of there, wrapped my wrist with a baby diaper, and took some aspirin for the pain. Bad idea! This thinned out my blood and made terrible blood clots and hematoma.

When we got home, I had to leave to speak at a VOM conference in Little Rock the next day. I figured I would be just as miserable no matter where I was, so I got on the plane for Houston. I had a terrible time with my briefcase and suitcase because neither one of my arms would work. The broken ribs were all on my right side, and my left wrist was cracked all the way across. Then I made the mistake of lying down when I finally got to the hotel room. I could not get back up. I was scared to call 911 and go to the hospital, because I had no US medical insurance. Somehow I rolled over onto the floor and got up but was unable to lie down for the rest of the trip. A brother from Pakistan, Mujihad, roomed with me, and after he prayed for me, I was able to make it back to Colombia. At home, Marina ordered me to the doctor who found that one of the ribs had stopped just short of puncturing my right lung. The doctor really couldn't do much, he just ordered a brace for my wrist. I was able to keep flying the Pink Panther, as my flight physical was not due for several more months.

Typically, I would leave home at 2:00 a.m. and drive to Sumapaz under the cover of darkness. Luis made me a garage of rough sawn lumber, and I would hide my truck in the garage at the crack of dawn. The horses would be ready, and I could disappear up into the mountains for days without worrying that someone might try to ambush me as I returned to my vehicle. Then on the way back, I would wait until dark in order to leave. Many people are scared to travel up there in the dark. For me, it is the other way around, because most bandits sleep in and do not get up early, and in the evening they start drinking and lose interest in what is coming down the road. At any rate, the Lord has kept me safe on hundreds of these trips all over some of the most delicate areas of Colombia. In fact, in rugged mountainous areas where the weather was terrible or where it was impossible to get permission to overfly the area, we could always drive around the back roads after midnight, throwing parachutes out the back of the truck. The people would think that they came down from the sky!

I came home from one of these extended journeys, picked up my boys, Dylan and Russ Jr., from school and went to the airport. We fired up our Pink Panther Cessna 180 and took off for the coastal city of Santa Marta where Marina awaited us for a vacation. Immediately after takeoff, we hit turbulence in the clouds and were approaching icing conditions as we crossed the Andes out of Bogotá, but we finally broke out and descended into the Magdalena River Valley. Our new baby Golden Retriever, Lucy, was with Dylan in the back seat.

Soon, I was sitting by the side of a pool in a resort city, a different world. My two cell phones were constantly ringing with calls from people on all different sides of the conflict responding to our gospel messages, or asking us to please come and see them or they wanted Bibles or radios or they were sick or wounded or... As I fumbled to shift gears and spend some quality time with my family, somehow I ended up in the swimming pool with my cell phones still in my pocket. Sammy tried to help me dry them off, but to no avail. The unit we were staying in had a nice microwave, so I decided to attempt to use it to dry out my precious cell phones. There was an explosion and a shower of sparks. That was the end of my phones. Now I could concentrate on my family for the rest of our vacation.

My wife, Marina, is not fond of flying, but I managed to convince her to return to Bogotá with us in the Pink Panther. We were about half way home to Bogotá on the three-and-a-half-hour flight, when disaster struck again. We were cruising along at 11,500 feet with the special turbochargers fully engaged which greatly boosted our speed. As the Magdalena Valley began to narrow, flanked by high mountains of the central ridge of the Andes on our right and by a military no-fly zone on our left, a strange cloud formation blocked our way. One of our two allowed alternates was already weathered in with thunderstorms. Our second alternate was on the other side of the cloud formation. The only other choice would be to return two hours flying time to Santa Marta to the site of our departure and try again the next day.

I looked at the storm scope and could see no T-cell activity. So I decided to poke our nose into the clouds with the idea that if it got too bad, we could always turn around and go back. Russ Jr. was in the co-pilot's seat. Dylan, Marina, Gabriella (our small granddaughter), and Lucy were all in the back seat. When we entered the cloud, it was like hitting a wall. Turning around was completely out of the question. I began to ease the power back as the plane was thrown into a violent twisting updraft. I wondered if our instruments were correct. Airspeed was way too high and our vertical speed was pegged. I had to put in almost full left aileron, vainly trying to keep the Cessna right side up while doubts raced through my mind that maybe our attitude gyro had failed.

By this time, there was a lot of noise coming out of the back seat as Marina screamed and pounded on my back. Dylan was yelling pretty loud too, but the howls of Lucy, our four-month-old puppy pierced over the top of everything. Russ Jr. was silent and followed me through on the controls, which I had told him to do because I thought he might learn something. He undoubtedly did.

In much less than a minute, it was over. We had been thrown almost two thousand feet up and exited the cloud with the wings at almost ninety degrees in spite of all the aileron I was holding against the rotation. Later I figured it must have been a horizontal rotor cloud, which is like a huge tornado going sideways. We must have hit it at about a 45-degree angle toward the bottom of the side with the lift. If we had hit it coming the other way, we could have been dashed into the rugged terrain below.

Years later, when we decommissioned the Pink Panther and sent it to be on display in Bartlesville at VOM headquarters, we had to remove the wing bolts with a sledgehammer. The bolts came out bent and starting to crack. If I had not reduced power, the airplane would have probably come apart. Yet if we had been much slower, I might have lost control of the airplane, and it would have flipped over on its back. For the rest of the years that we operated the airplane, I always did the maneuvers slow and easy with minimum g-forces when we were dropping parachutes. Somehow, each time I thought I would really put the airplane through its paces, as I do from time to time on just about all our other aircraft, I would feel a gentle nudge in my spirit to take it easy. So the 1953 airplane made it through its last years of service with two damaged wing bolts and damaged wing root spars but without critical structural failure.

# CHAPTER 5

# Missionary Aviation

I started fixing up a two-place PA-18 Super Cub that had replaced our ultralight. Then I figured that it would make a great spray plane trainer. Since Ag planes are not so tightly controlled, it could be a good way to drop parachutes in delicate areas where it was difficult to fly the Pink Panther. A good friend of mine, Jairo Gaitan, was retiring as an ag instructor at the mandatory age of sixty-five (for Colombia). He had a few days left before his birthday when I found out that there was no one on the horizon to take his place.

To be an ag instructor in Colombia is a high honor and pretty much a closed club. Every spray pilot in the country has to have a yearly check ride and evaluation, and every new ag pilot has to have a course with forty-four hours of flight instruction.

Since I had previous experience spraying with both fixed-wing and helicopter and because of our friendship, Jairo agreed to check me out as an instructor. The only problem was that the local Civil Aviation Authority Office told us that we would have to go to Bogotá and receive special permission to go ahead with our plans. This could take weeks, and Jairo's instructor license would expire in just a few days. We were still having this discussion in the regional office when an airplane landed. The head of the National Aviation License Office stepped out and walked over to us. It turned out he had read my book and always wanted to meet me. He authorized us to do a few hours of training and then a check ride with the local government examiner.

As we were flying around in the spray plane doing the checkout, Jairo decided that we should fly under some electric power lines. When we went to pull up, I noticed that we had no oil pressure. Then we noticed that black engine oil was streaming down both sides of the airplane. It turned out our oil cooler had blown several leaks. Jairo knew of a nearby spray plane base, and we were able to make it, although the engine was toast. However, I did receive the coveted ag instructor license.

Jairo also owned a small charter airline, licensed to operate in Mitu, Vaupes. His airplanes are some of the only ones allowed to fly into the jungle airstrips abandoned years ago when all the mission aviation programs like Jungle Aviation and Radio Service (JAARS), Mission Aviation Fellowship (MAF), and New Tribes were forced to leave Colombia. Soon we began to make plans to restore air service to places that had not seen a missionary for twenty-five years.

The days of the typical mission airplane manned by North American pilots has long been over in Colombia. One of the JAARS airplanes was apparently sabotaged on its last flight to Mitu many years ago. It was a Helio Courier tail number HK 612, which was nicknamed Sick One Two because it was so underpowered. On takeoff from Mitu, pilot Tom Smoak reported that he lost power just before settling into 200-foot-tall trees. Everyone on board survived, thanks in part to the exceptional safety characteristics of the Helio, although there were some serious injuries. Later it was thought that while the airplane was on the ramp prior to takeoff, someone probably loosened the bolts holding the throttle mechanism, causing the airplane to lose power once it was in flight.

Another time the JAARS DC-3 parked on the ramp at the

Bogotá El Dorado Airport, right next to another DC-3 belonging to a cargo company in which a friend of mine was the co-pilot. In the middle of the night, someone put large handfuls of metal filings down the oil inlet on both engines of the cargo DC-3, apparently mistaking it for the JAARS plane, which may have been their real target.

The cargo DC-3 took off in the early morning with a full load when the co-pilot noticed the right engine temps were increasing and the oil pressure falling. The captain thought at first it was just faulty gauges. Then, the engine abruptly quit and the exact same thing happened to the left engine. They had been in the clouds, climbing out of Bogotá to the north and about to cross serious mountains. The captain was able to maintain proper altitude due to an electric emergency gyro that had been recently installed. The vacuum gyros all failed when the engines quit. They came out of the clouds a few hundred feet in the air in the center of the valley, lined up with a potato field, and landed with minimal damage. The co-pilot, however, had a mild nervous breakdown and was not able to fly again for several years.

We have had several incidents with our airplanes that likely were sabotage. The last involved both the oil cooler on the engine and the tail of the airplane, which had been welded to the airframe at an unsafe angle.

I can envision a new day of missionary aviation in Colombia in which we use aircraft that are part of local companies and not identified with North American mission agencies that make them stand out as terrorist targets. We are also training pilots and crew from among the local people. Hundreds of missionaries have left Colombia over the past twenty years. They are the ones who were paying for missionary aviation flight hours. Now, local pastors and evangelists have an even greater need for missionary aviation, but they do not have the same financial capability. After fifty years of war, if Colombia enters into successful peace, entire towns and villages will have to be rebuilt. Much restoration will need to take place. In addition to small 4- to 6-seat airplanes, we will need DC-3s, Twin Otters, and who knows? Maybe even 737s. Mitu now has a 5000-foot paved runway that can take a 737. This may require future aviation missionaries to expand our vision and run scheduled airline service, charter flights to oil companies, medevac flights, and other ventures in order to subsidize the missionary flying.

Our friend, Carl Mortenson, designed the twin engine Angel Aircraft for our exact situation. We are still praying we will be able to obtain at least two of these magnificent, short field, twin-engine missionary airplanes. (See www.angelaircraft.com).

Over the past several years, we have accumulated a growing number of small aircraft and have been training some promising young men and women. It takes a lot of time, money, patience, and determination to train good pilots so they are safe in the mountains and in the jungle. We also need to be sure God really has His hand on them so they will not fail in the midst of environments of extreme corruption and temptation.

We have managed to get books, Bibles, Galcom radios, and other materials into many remote, out-of-the-way places where the people are more and more open to the gospel. But there is no substitute for personal contact. There is a need to get back in on the ground to be able to have direct personal contact with the people. In the one-third of Colombia that is readily accessible only by air (and the same is true for Venezuela), missionary aviation is a wonderful way to serve the community. This is our vision for the future of Colombia and Venezuela and other countries.

# CHAPTER 6

## Steve

Even after being ousted, General Castellanos continued to recommend me to his friends who were still rising through the ranks in the Colombian Army. General Guillermo Quiñones was the commander of the 4th Division, and he welcomed me with open arms. I was sent over to the Apiai Air Force base in the general's personal vehicle and with his escorts to meet General Ulloa, the base commander. He and I hit it off and this led to a meeting in which I was asked to address all of his pilots.

At the same time, my close missionary friend, Ray Rising, who had been kidnapped for over two years, made friends with some Christian officers at the US Embassy who were military attachés and introduced them to me. They were very concerned about three American contractors who had been kidnapped by the FARC. At this time, there were a number of high-profile hostages including: Ingred Betacourt, who had been a presidential candidate; Allan Jara, the Governor of the Department of Meta; a number of Colombian military personnel, as well as hundreds of businessmen, ranchers, and politicians.

I proposed to all the powers that be that I be allowed to drop parachutes with Galcom solar radios on likely spots I thought might be near any of the hostages. I was soon given freedom to fly wherever I needed to go. A ship loaded thousands of Galcom radios and brought them discreetly into Colombia. Many years later, by the time all the hostages finally escaped, were rescued, or were released, virtually all of them had encountered our radios. Some told of how they spent five, six, or even eight years under a triple jungle canopy, carefully placing the radios under any available sunbeam so they would be able to listen to us at night. They would have to move the radio every few minutes as the angle of the sun was constantly changing.

Chaddy and I made another trip to the Sumapaz paramo high country. We found Noel and some of his friends just as a huge military operation attacked them. Bombs were falling, and I was amazed how many of them seemed to be duds. The guerrillas would offer rewards to the campesinos to hunt for unexploded 250-pound bombs which would then be dug up and cut open by the guerrillas who craved the explosive. One unexploded bomb could provide for hundreds of small home-made anti-personnel mines manufactured by the FARC and designed with just enough force to blow a person's foot off.

We were forced to retreat back into the mountains with Noel as he personally accompanied us to keep us out of the crossfire. This brought us into contact with hundreds of guer-rillas that we would never have met otherwise. Chaddy and I had to shoulder our backpacks, and Noel's men drove our horses down the extreme footpaths that seemed like they were designed for mountain goats. Somehow our horses went over the obstacles and down almost perpendicular slopes without breaking a leg. We spent several nights under the cover of thin trees with government bombers circling overhead, wondering if the next bomb would hit the camp we were in. After a couple of days through a maze of tangled wilderness, we were glad to get back on an established mule trail where we could once again mount our horses. Even then, mine slipped over the side of a small cliff, and I had to bail out. Again we were able to retrieve the horse, and it was not injured.

All of this tired out the horses as we tried to get all the speed we could out of them to outflank the fighting and get safely back to the road where we had left our vehicle. Eventually I had to switch to a spare horse which was not mountain-bred and was barely broke for riding. It began to rain as we traversed a very slippery high slope that was like a black peat bog. My horse became nervous and began to buck until it lost its balance and went over the side. I bailed out, but the only option was on the downside, which was a long fall. Fortunately, I hit in the soft muck. But then, out of the corner of my eye, I saw the horse coming down, end over end on top of me. With only a split second, I turned sideways so the mare hit me square on my hips, and I missed getting creamed by the saddle. Chaddy could not believe it when I jumped up, caught the wild horse, and got back on. Every few minutes, he kept asking me if I was okay because he imagined that after such a blow I must have been hemorrhaging internally. By the grace of God, I got out of that one and only had some massive bruises.

When we hit the main road, Chaddy and our guide and two others were way up ahead when some soldiers seemingly came out of nowhere and tried to stop them. My wild horse took the bit in its teeth and charged down the road at a full gallop. It went through the group of soldiers like a powerful fullback hitting the line of scrimmage in a football game. I had my hat in my right hand, the reigns in my left, all my weight back in the stirrups in a desperate futile attempt to get the bit loose. The horse slowed slightly and was pounding hard, skidding sideways. The soldiers scattered into both ditches, and then one yelled to his friends, "Get him, that's the blond guy we have been hunting for six months!" When I heard them confuse me with one of the guerrillas, I gave the horse its head and spurred it on full blast. Chaddy and our guides did the same, and we all disappeared around a bend in the road before the soldiers could fire a shot.

One of the points Noel had mentioned as we brainstormed about how to end the war was that even though he had orders to not give any interviews to Colombian national news media, he was allowed to speak on the record to international news media. So I told him about my journalist friend, Steven Salisbury, who had written a great article about me that was published in the *Washington Times* on December 10, 2002, titled "In Colombia, a Mission for Peace." Noel encouraged me to bring Steve out to see him, and we set a date.

About this time, some amazing events took place that involved our Christian friends at the US Embassy, General Quiñiones, and other key individuals who must remain unnamed. These were the real heroes. The official name for what happened was Operacion *Jaque* (Checkmate). I called the real version a Long Bomb Hail Mary Pass in which the guerrillas were outfoxed and most of the high-profile hostages including the three Americans were rescued. The truth can be summed up in two words: God intervened.

Steve was very enthusiastic and went with me back out into the Sumapaz high country right as the Hail Mary Pass was launched. In fact, our trip may have diverted the attention of the guerrilla leadership right when they were getting blindsided. We met with Noel and Reynaldo at the remote house of some dear campesinos who had befriended me for a long time. They had an elderly friend we called El Abuelo (Grandfather) who had come to the Lord. He was illiterate, and I had given him a MegaVoice solar-powered audio Bible to which he spent most of his spare time listening. A month or so later on my next trip, I was very sad to learn that El Abuelo had accidentally stepped on a large mine set by the guerrillas and was blown to smithereens. It made me wonder how many times I may have come very close to the same fate without even knowing it.

Steve was very professional with the interview and able to

glean important details that would prove to be extremely valuable to help set the stage for peace talks that would take place well into the future, which is now. One important point was when they said they were tired of talks with corrupt politicians and they wanted to negotiate directly with the generals, who were their counterparts in the war.

It would be very difficult to get a story from Colombia on the front page of major newspapers, but Steve thought we might have a chance. We had brought along a box of interesting little trinkets, books, movies, etc. to share with people along the way as icebreakers. It was election time in the United States, and we had a McCain campaign tee shirt and an Obama tee shirt. It did not take long for two of the guerrillas to put on the tee shirts. Then, we helped them make a big sign by taping four posters together so they could write a message across the back. I helped them translate their message into English so they could write it on the sign. It said, "We Want Change and Respect Too, Friends Plan, FARC-EP." I was helping the two of them get the sign between them with their AK-47s in their opposite hands and did not notice when Steve clicked a nice shot with me in the frame.

Steve noted the great attitude and cordial behavior of Noel and all of his men and women. I explained that this was because they had been profoundly touched by the love and presence of God. It was very evident they were all seeking a way to end the war with honor and dignity.

As we rode our horses six hours back to our truck, Steve was impressed at the number of rabbits the dogs were able to hunt. Oso scarfed the first one up in what looked like a single gulp. Then they started bringing us the dead rabbits.

It was hard to stay on the horses in the slippery, treacherous conditions, and I was worried we might get thrown off into big rocks or over the side. When we finally made it back to the road, the face of the mule I was riding was plastered with mud. The mule had gone face down in the mud on several occasions as we went down steep inclines laced with obstacles. Each time, I was able to stay in the saddle, and eventually the valiant animal would get up with me still on board and keep going.

When Steve wrote his article, the *Washington Times* did not initially want to run it. He wrote me an email asking for permission to use my name, as he felt this was the only way to convince the editors. I thought about it and told Steve to go ahead. The *Miami Herald*, and *El Nuevo Herald*, took the story. I was amazed to see the picture of me standing between the two guerrillas in their McCain and Obama tee shirts on the front page of the paper. That was nothing, however, compared to when the Miami paper released the story and photo in Spanish (July 20, 2008, *El Nuevo Herald*). It made the front page of over a dozen very influential Spanish newspapers all over the world as well as Colombia. Steve estimated that over 30 million people saw that picture. Suddenly, TV reporters showed up wanting to interview me. I had to take off for Canada to speak at a summer camp and let things die down.

When I got back to Colombia a few days later, Paco Mejia took me to see General Herrazo, who came over to our house and looked at other pictures of me with the guerrillas, including one with me standing beside Aldinever – who is known as Zarco because of his clear blue-green eyes. He was Noel's immediate commander and was in charge of at least five guerrilla fronts (or battalions). The message about the guerrillas wanting to talk to the generals had apparently hit home. Now General Montoya, the commander of the Colombian Army, wanted to see me. We began to work out the details for secret, coded communications between the two sides at a very high level. But I was to learn that the idea of a negotiated peace was definitely not the first priority of General Montoya, who participated in the firing of

General Quiñiones not long after Operation Checkmate. Maybe they did not want to give Quiñiones the credit he deserved.

I was asked to go back out, find Noel, and give him a message. Little did I know, I was being tracked. When I got back to the house where Steve and I did the interview, there were camouflaged Special Forces' sharp shooters on the opposite slope waiting patiently to get Noel into their cross hairs. It took a couple of days for me to make contact with the guerrillas, and the soldiers got hungry. A couple of men on the sniper team snuck out backwards to a farmhouse, where they purchased some chickens and then returned to their positions. Just about everyone in the area loved and trusted me. Soon I was clued in.

When I found out the extreme danger we were in, it was about 5:00 p.m. and would soon be dark. Knowing I was being closely observed, I acted nonchalant while I prayed about what to do. Slightly after 6:00 p.m., as the light in the deep valley was fading fast, Elias, one of Noel's company commanders who was black, slipped in the back door of the cabin alone.

I was pretty sure he had been undetected by the sniper team, so I made sure Elias stayed out of sight while we talked for a few minutes. Then Elias disappeared into the now pitch black night. Unbelievably, the guerrilla high command had taken issue with Noel over the interview – never mind that their positive message had hit the front page of all the major newspapers in the Spanish-speaking world and that it had aired on many TV news programs. No, they had removed Noel from his command and sanctioned him because they thought he was influencing internal politics in the United States with the McCain and Obama tee shirts. Steve and I had thought this made it balanced. Apparently Mono Jojoy, the top FARC military commander who was brilliant but had a second grade level education, thought differently.

In fact, time would tell that it was impossible to negotiate with him. Upon his death, the very pragmatic Mauricio Jaramillo, known as the Doctor, took his place, and at the invitation of President Santos, helped set the stage and agenda for the present Peace Negotiations in Cuba.

The good part about this amazing setback was that it most likely saved the life of Noel. If he had walked into that clearing in broad daylight to greet me, as was his custom, he would have most certainly been killed. And who knows what might have happened to me in the crossfire or if any of the other guerrilla commanders in the area might have blamed me for what would have happened?

Other serious incidents followed. Two soldiers somehow got away from their unit and started drinking beer in the local store near where I had parked my truck. A nasty guerrilla nicknamed One Ear, who was the explosives expert, was drinking at the next table. He feigned friendship with the soldiers and bought them more beer. They all moved to the same table. One Ear sent a kid to fetch his pistol, which was brought to him in a bag. The storekeeper unexpectedly came home and was so shocked at the fact that his sister had been serving beer to all these characters that he kicked them all out of the store.

One Ear also had a bottle of *Aguardiente* (firewater) in his bag. So he pulled that out and went down the road, proffering toasts and offering swigs out of his bottle to the confused soldiers until he was able to pull out his pistol and shoot both of them in the head. One of the bullets went through the head of the soldier and hit one of my guides – who just happened to be in the wrong place at the wrong time – in the arm. He went back to the house we were using for our base, trailing blood. One Ear stripped the uniforms and weapons from the dead soldiers and then continued down the road, drinking his firewater and firing an occasional burst into the air from one of his new assault rifles.

A huge investigation followed, which could have tainted us. When he sobered up, One Ear deserted from the guerrilla ranks, fearing a court martial for acting in such a way without orders. We weren't able to continue using the location. Fortunately, Paco Mejia and General Herrazo believed me when I insisted all of our people were innocent.

Noel was eventually reinstated to his command. We were able to return to the area and continue to build our radio station.

But there was a lot of chaos on all sides, and the episode with One Ear was typical. It was normal for conscript soldiers to walk into general stores, fill their canteens with beer, and pay for it with ammunition or hand grenades that the storekeeper would sell to the guerrillas. Paco Mejia was very concerned. He also wanted to know where the guerrillas were getting all the explosives. It was not just mines; car bombs were also common, and Paco knew that some were in the works and in fact, way overdue. I told him the only way to really stop this was if God would directly intervene and I was going to ask him. Paco looked at me kind of strange.

A few days later, there was a huge grass fire behind the general store where the drinking episode had taken place. A nearby battalion of soldiers helped put it out and saved some farmhouses. Near the end of the fire, there were two huge explosions when two big stashes of explosives, apparently destined for car bombs, got set off by the fire. I called Paco and told him that God had just intervened according to our request. The nearby soldiers were able to verify this.

A few months later, international journalists did a flurry of reporting about a scandal related to false positives and implicated General Montoya. He was forced to resign from the Army and exiled to an embassy in the Caribbean. Over-zealous officers had been rounding up unemployed young men and bums, taking them out to the mountains and jungles where they were subsequently shot and passed off as guerrillas. Then the body count was reported as enemy deaths to bolster the personnel file of certain key officers in order to secure promotion and reward money – literal blood money.

# CHAPTER 7

# Eduardo Robayo and Jon Dufendach

After several years of disconnect, I received a call from Eduardo Robayo, one of the three guerrilla commanders portrayed in the movie, *La Montana*. He told me he was stationed in the southern part of the Department of Guaviare and wanted me to come and see him. So I went with my friend Henry Tequia.

Henry was similar to Ever, except Henry came from the guerrilla militia side of things. Before his conversion, Henry had trafficked up and down most of the rivers and back roads of Guaviare, southern Meta, and quite a few other places. Henry also had a big dose of wanderlust from his Gypsy background. I have given Henry large amounts of Bibles, literature, and radios to distribute in difficult guerrilla areas, and he has always done an excellent job.

We went through San Jose del Guaviare before dawn and took the back roads used by drug growers to get to San Luis without going through the paramilitary roadblocks between El Retorno and Calamar. Then we went on to La Cristalina where we met the guerrilla contact man sent by Eduardo. Whenever we would stop somewhere, the people would take one look at me and mutter to one another that Henry must be leading me into danger. They fully expected me to be kidnapped and disappear for a long, long time.

Eduardo had been through the mill since I had last seen him. He had been seriously wounded at least two times due to his very aggressive behavior in combat. He had also been promoted. After a joyful greeting, I was introduced to Yesid, his immediate superior, and we also became great friends. Eduardo and Yesid authorized us to distribute our literature, Bibles, and radios in their area. Henry and I joyfully drove home passing out copies of *Rescue the Captors* to the people in all the little farms and hamlets.

We made many trips into this area. After a while, one of the communist militia leaders called Eduardo aside. He said, "Something terrible is going on in your area that has to be a unique case in the FARC. There is a Gringo loose in this area that comes and goes as he pleases. He rides around in a big red truck and then disappears into the jungle for days. Then he unexpectedly shows up out of nowhere, covered with mud, jumps back in his truck and leaves!"

Eduardo smiled and replied, "I am not sure who you are referring to, but I want to you to understand something. In this guerrilla unit, we are not monsters. If someone does not owe us anything, they do not have to pay us anything. If this person can come and go so freely, don't you think there must be a special reason?"

Henry and Eduardo and Yesid all became excellent friends. God began to touch people for miles around. Ana Tulia was a very religious person who wound up demon-possessed at a revival camp meeting of a pastor who had a demonic religious spirit instead of the real Holy Spirit. Every now and then, a horrible look would appear in her eyes, and she would attempt to kill people, even her own family. For miles around, everyone was terrified of her. So the pastor used her to collect tithe money from the local drug growers. On one of our trips through the area to visit Eduardo, Henry and I left some radios, books, and Bibles with Pastor Carlos, thinking he was probably okay and would freely give out the material. He lived right on the edge of the last place where the communists allowed pastors and churches. Even so he was expected to pay them money.

The pastor then sold one of our radios to Ana Tulia in exchange for two of her last chickens. She was drawn to the messages and wanted to meet me. One day she flagged me down as I was returning from San Miguel. I only had a few minutes before dark, and I had to make tracks because government aircraft might shoot at any vehicle moving after dark in a guerrilla area. I handed her a few more radios and the first copy of a new book, *Extreme Devotion,* I had just received from VOM and I left. She told me later that when I put those materials into her hands, the demons that had been causing her so much trouble for so many years all left and she felt the sweet presence of the real Holy Spirit.

Soon Ana Tulia was a powerhouse for God. The wives of all the local drug growers, guerrilla commanders, and drug lords started helping her pass out the materials. Then government spray planes eradicated most of the drug fields, and hard times descended on the area. Soon Pastor Carlos noticed that when the people started listening to our radios and when they came into direct contact with God, he could not control them any longer. Furious, he ran around trying to destroy the radios. Yesid heard about this and went over and had a firm talk with Carlos. Yesid gave the pastor an ultimatum: No more radios were to be destroyed. A few days later, when Ana Tulia told me what had happened, she exclaimed, "And I know that God really touched Yesid because he did not even shoot that pastor!"

People started clamoring for me to come and hold meetings. If a rumor started that I would purportedly be at a certain place at a certain time, large numbers of people would congregate in expectation. Ana Tulia pleaded with me to allow her to schedule speaking events. The answer that I got from the Lord was no. People could listen to me on the radio and read my books. If we started large meetings too soon, we would have to set up leadership, and the people were still too immature. Look at Pastor Carlos! Meetings would also set off a lot of jealousy and undoubtedly cause problems for Eduardo and Yesid.

An old friend from Alaska, Jon Dufendach, came down to see us. He looked over our Lomalinda radio station and said it was fine, but he wanted to see the results. Where were the local congregations? Where were the elders and pastors who would shepherd each flock? Did we have any visible, tangible results?

I thought for a minute and told Jon, "The only way to communicate what is happening to you would be to take you back into the difficult areas where the people are listening to our radio signals. And to take an American who does not speak Spanish is serious, but you are a very wealthy businessman and that is even more serious. You could even get into trouble with the government for trying to go into a rebel zone."

Jon decided to go. We got up at 2:00 a.m. and got through San Jose under cover of darkness without hitting any roadblocks. Then we threaded our way through the rundown back roads that had deteriorated substantially since the heydays of the drug business. We arrived at Ana Tulia's house about noon. As people drifted in and out of the house, Jon could tell by the smiles on their faces and the look in their eyes that the real Holy Spirit was at work. The next day, we drove in four-wheel drive to the end of an extremely rough road to an abandoned farmhouse. Eduardo was waiting for us. Jon saw him put down his rifle, stand it in a corner, and come forward with a huge smile on his face to give us each a hug.

I translated a most interesting conversation between them.

Jon told Eduardo about how he had served in the US Army during the Vietnam war and how much he had hated the communists. Eduardo told Jon about how much he used to hate Americans. Jon said, "God told me this morning, before I even met you, that He has called you to be a peacemaker. What do you think about that?"

"Yes," replied Eduardo, and there was a tear in his eye.

Jon owns a water purification company in Alaska called Camp Water. He has installed water purification units of all different sizes and capabilities in many countries. He had a unit in the back of my truck that he showed Eduardo. Eduardo told him most of the sickness and disease in his area, including many deaths, came from drinking bad water. The two men became instant friends. Jon tried his unit out in a nearby creek where the water ran brown. It came out of his machine crystal clear. Alethia was along to help, so Jon named it Alethia Creek. Then Jon set up his Camp Water company in Bogotá with everything needed to make his two smallest designs and signed it over to us so that the proceeds finance the ministry. Sammy's dad, Anibal, runs the company, and we now have water purification units scattered all over Colombia. We have a program called, "A Pure Word and Clean Water."

After a while, Eduardo got transferred to command the 42nd Front (Giovani's old unit) behind the Macarena Mountains. He continued to develop spiritually and was a great blessing to all around him. I started having problems with bandits, with corrupt law enforcement, false accusations, and many other troubles. Eduardo was given orders to stamp out some new churches that were invading his area even if he had to kill the pastors. Some of them were what most of us would probably consider to be cults. I got desperate messages to come and visit even as it got more and more impossible for me to travel over there. Then we got the news: Eduardo had been betrayed and shot by his enemies. Jon Dufendach and I are confident that we will see him again someday in heaven.

Colonel Robinson got promoted again, this time to brigadier general. His first post was San Jose del Guaviare. We were able to work together and plaster most of his area with parachutes loaded with books, Bibles, and radios. Robinson, like Barrero, perfectly understood that in order to consolidate peace, it was not enough to militarily win. Hearts must change. Attitudes must change. General Robinson wanted help with several new Christian radio stations.

One of my engineers named Juan had climbed up a tower at one of Robinson's outposts and was installing the antenna when the guerrillas attacked. Juan stayed up there and finished the job amid a hail of bullets. The captain in the bunker below handed Abel his assault rifle and opened up on the rebels who were hiding behind tombstones. His 81-millimeter mortar blew a huge hole in the local cemetery and sent the guerrillas scrambling back into the jungle.

Back at Ana Tulia's neck of the woods, some bad doctrine misled Yesid. He started to listen to Pastor Carlos who talked about no real need for repentance and that God will not condemn us for doing whatever we are pressured to do. Yesid and his men and women continued to do some very awful things because they were following orders and this is what they had always done. Carlos told them that as long as they believed in God and prayed they would be okay.

Ana Tulia woke up one morning with a horrible feeling. She went and found Yesid and told him she had a message from God that he and his unit were to repent. Swift judgment was on the way. There was no time to lose. Yesid shrugged her off and went back to his camp. That night, the camp was bombed, killing everyone except Yesid. Ana Tulia found him in his underwear, distraught and wandering around in circles in a cow pasture with his eardrums and balance affected from the blast. She took him to safety and clothed him in some of her husband's clothing before Army helicopters came in at dawn to mop up. A new guerrilla unit was sent to the area, and Yesid was recalled to guerrilla headquarters. As she finished telling me what happened, Anna Tulia said, "And this time, I think Yesid might really become converted!"

And then I got an urgent phone call. It was Pastor Carlos. He said he was in a lot of trouble and in desperate need of my advice. He confessed he had stashed a box of Richard Wurmbrand books under his bed. Henry had given them to him many years ago. There was one with a nice picture of Karl Marx on the front (In English it is called *Marx and Satan,* but in Spanish we renamed it *The Unknown Marx.*), and he had pulled one out and put it on his coffee table. However, in the almost ten years he had the box of books he had never read it.

A new guerrilla commander had come by, and unlike Yesid, this one was extremely antagonistic to the gospel. The commander had fallen in love with the nice picture of Marx on the cover of the book, so Carlos gave it to him. Then, feeling uneasy, he got another copy of the book out of the box under his bed and started to read it. He had not read very far before he called me, horrified, wondering how much trouble he was in. What did I think? Would the guerrilla commander come back and shoot him? Should he flee?

I tried to keep from laughing as I gave him the best advice I could. I told him the best thing that could happen to him would be if he could put his life on the line for the Lord. I encouraged him to read the entire book and be prepared to answer his questions when he returns. "He may be mad, but he may not kill you just over one book. And never, ever do anything like this again without being genuinely led by the Spirit of God."

# CHAPTER 8

# Walter and Carrillo

An epic battle royal continued to rage across the high, rugged terrain of Sumapaz that looked like scenes out of Rohan in the movie *The Lord of The Rings*. Rain, sleet, and even snow made it miserable for those on all sides. Some died of hypothermia. Everyone had to have two sets of clothes, one in a waterproof plastic bag to wear at night and the other, which would almost always be damp and wet to wear in the daytime. Once you put on the stiff, wet clothes in the early morning, the only way to survive was to keep moving and burn as many calories as possible. By now we had radio repeaters broadcasting from the tops of several huge mountains down into regions of intense spiritual darkness that seemed like the land of Mordor.

Both sides had huge supply problems. Army helicopters could not operate with heavy loads at such high altitudes. They could barely keep up with removing the wounded, many who had stepped on land mines. Occasionally, a guerrilla would get confused and step on one of their own mines. Soldiers would stagger around at 13,000 feet with 80- to 100-pound packs, which could only support them for about a week. Under those conditions, they could only move a few thousand meters per day. I started finding huge piles of hundreds of empty rum bottles wherever the Army had camped for any extended amount of time. An officer, who wished to remain anonymous, confirmed that the only way to keep the morale of the soldiers up in such tough conditions was to give them each a bottle or two of rum whenever they were supplied. Sometimes the guerrillas did the same, but with Aguardiente (firewater). I took some pictures of all the cans and bottles littered over the pristine wilderness and showed them to Paco and the general. Soon the Army cleaned up its act.

The guerrillas were masters at using mule supply trains to the end of a trail, and then they would carry heavy loads on their shoulders for days back into the rugged labyrinth of sharp peaks, crevices, and tight canyons of what has to be one of the most difficult pieces of vertical real estate in the world. Soon the Army was using mules also. The vast Alpine meadows, like tundra above the timber line, rolled for miles and miles, ending in deep, tight valleys that went down into miserable tangles of dense underbrush, followed by very intense jungle under about ten thousand feet elevation.

Sometimes I would encounter up to forty pack mules with ten or twenty armed guerrillas on horses escorting their precious cargo. The mules would form an emotional bond with the horses and follow them without having to be driven. All of them would go at a brisk trot, and maybe even a gallop, thundering across the tundra to keep from being stopped by the Army before they could disappear after a few hours into some type of deep and impossible terrain. On occasion, loaded pack mules and even horses with empty saddles would get mixed up, and animals belonging to the guerrillas would wind up at an Army outpost or vice versa.

Intelligence aircraft and sometimes drones were almost always overhead. At first the aircraft had to fly back to home base in order to develop and analyze the film from their hi-tech, three-dimensional cameras. Later in the war, they were able to relay hi-res information in real time back to Army command and control centers, and the bombers could be in the air close by, capable of dropping a smart bomb instantly onto any available target.

Hilber and I were in the middle of crossing a thirty-mile stretch of Alpine meadow one day when we came to a chasm that was only about four or five feet across at the top, but underneath it widened out and had a rushing torrent in the bottom almost forty feet below. We decided to dismount, jump across the chasm holding the lead ropes of our horses, and then coax them across. Everything went fine until my horse panicked, reared, and then made a wild leap. Its front feet made it to the opposite side, but in the confusion it had not left enough room for the hind feet, which went down the chasm. I had my camera in my hand and had to make an instant choice between filming what would have been a hit video on YouTube or helping Hilber in his desperate attempt to save the horse.

At the time, it was a no-brainer. The horse was rented and expensive. I threw down the camera and grabbed a piece of the lead rope that extended through Hilber's capable hands. It was to no avail. The horse kept going down the chasm. But for some reason, we had quite a long lead rope, which reached all the way to the bottom. I can still remember the horrible sight of the horse thrashing around in the bottom in the midst of huge boulders as it was sucked down the raging torrent. Hilber, however, did not give up and ran along the edge of the chasm still hanging on to the lead rope until after about a hundred and fifty yards, the chasm ended and turned into a broad stream surrounded by deep mud similar to quicksand.

By this time, the horse had gone completely limp from exhaustion and from the beating it had taken coming down that awful chute. It was all we could do to hold its head above water without us getting sucked into the quicksand. In the midst of an intense battle that lasted almost an hour, we managed to get the saddle off and float the horse down the icy stream to a place that had a shallow, firm bank. I was amazed when it got to its feet and stood there trembling. It was out of the question for me to continue riding it. We took the saddle and put it on the pack mule. Then Hilber rode the mule and gave me his horse. We left my horse behind to recover.

There were low clouds and light rain turning into sleet. And during most of this episode, we could hear what sounded like an intelligence aircraft or drone turning circles a couple thousand feet over our heads up in the clouds. They had probably detected us with their infrared heat sensors and were trying to figure out who we were and what was going on. I still wonder what they thought. Fortunately, they did not bomb us. Three days later, we returned and found the horse within a hundred yards of where we left it, happily eating clover and sweet grass beside the stream. Hilber saddled it up, and I rode it home. The next day Hilber returned it to its owner and paid the rent.

Every trip was unique, and on about every tenth trip or so, I would take Alethia or someone else with me. The responsibility weighed on me, however, because I instinctively knew how dangerous all this was. The people were extremely suspicious of outsiders, yet I wanted my friends and family to have an idea of what was going on and to be a part of every aspect of the ministry. It was on a trip like this when I found Walter. There were many opportunities to be a Good Samaritan, but Walter was over the top. A bomb blast had fractured several discs in his back. And on top of this, his hip socket was severely damaged with undue pressure on the sciatic nerve.

Even so, he had continued to walk and keep up with his comrades until he became virtually paralyzed with constant and unbearable pain. They had carried him on their shoulders for four days over impossible foot trails and then another two days tied to a mule like cargo with a nurse injecting morphine every few hours. In times past, I suspect the policy was to simply take people like this off to one side away from the camp and put them out of their misery with a *tiro de gracia* (a shot of grace).

But the guerrilla leaders had heard that I liked to help people, even seemingly impossible situations, and that I was trustworthy. So Walter had been sent to me. I went and got Dr. Fernando and the red truck. Dylan came along with his bow and arrows, planning to hunt rabbits along the way. Dr. Fernando said he was tired and went to sleep in the back seat. By the time we got there, I realized there was something wrong with the doctor. I thought altitude sickness at the time, but soon discovered it was really the beginning of some heart trouble that would require several extended hospital stays.

We took Walter home with us and put him in our boy's bedroom. There was no way we could take him to the hospital because he had no legal ID papers. Ray Rising, who was living next door, took turns with me staying up all night and injecting Walter with more morphine. Walter looked like a lean, mean, nasty, stray wolf with a wary, cornered look in his eyes. Marina came home and found Walter in the boys' room and was not very happy, and this is putting it mildly. I explained about overcoming evil with good. She said fine, but not in her house! The legal implications could be enormous if we were caught. I had a tacit agreement with friends in authority like Paco Mejia where they would let me do certain things and agree to cover me, but this was really stretching it.

Yet, what else could we do? There was no way to take him back and nowhere else to put him. After a couple of weeks of having an intensive care unit in our house, we found a doctor who would operate on him. First we had to have an MRI scan. I sent him down with Sammy, Sammy's dad (to pray), and my video engineer. They used the ID card of our engineer to register for the medical procedure. Finally, a nurse came out and called out the name of the patient. Walter went nuts! Walter was obviously not his real name but an alias. However, the first and last names called out by the nurse, which were the names of our engineer, turned out to be Walter's real names also.

They put him into the huge MRI machine while the nurse asked Walter to explain what had happened to him. He claimed that he had been bucked off a mule out at a ranch in the mountains and had hurt his back. When the exam was over and after a substantial wait, the nurse came back out holding the film with a puzzled look on her face and said, "If he fell off a mule, how come there is shrapnel all through his body?" The MRI was lit up like a Christmas tree. It looked like the medical people might call the police. Everyone prayed. The lights went out. A few minutes later when the power came back on, Walter, our guys, and all the results from the MRI were nowhere to be found.

The doctor decided to do micro back surgery on Walter with new equipment that had just been installed in one of the best hospitals in Bogotá. We were warned that the operation entailed substantial risk. Again, we had to sign Walter into the hospital with the ID card of our engineer. If Walter had died while under the extremely delicate operation our poor engineer would have been legally dead!

Walter eventually was able to return to the jungle, but would never really be up to the rigors of warfare in the mountains. So, it was decided by a top guerrilla commander – and Noel had no knowledge of this – that Walter and Carillo should return to Bogotá, find me, and pretend to sympathize with Christianity and defect. Then they were to worm their way into our confidence and use us as cover for terrorist activities in the city. Whoever dreamed this up obviously had absolutely no fear of the Lord (which is the beginning of wisdom).

On the hike from the guerrilla camp to the nearest road, Carillo stepped on a guerrilla mine and blew off his foot. Walter had to carry him back to camp with his bad back. They frantically called me for help, but I was far away on a trip. There was a gynecologist who worked at a hospital in the nearest town who was used to coming out to the guerrilla camp to perform abortions, as no children were allowed there. They called him, and he got into his little jeep and began speeding down the highway toward the guerrilla camp. The abortion doctor lost control on a tight curve, ran off the road, and killed himself.

After the guerrillas found out about the death of the abortion doctor, they called a Mafioso friend of theirs. He came out and got Walter and Carillo and took them to a hospital. They stayed with him quite a while and drank up most of the money that had been given them by the guerrilla movement to buy a legitimate business as a front. Then they tried to recoup their losses by investing the rest of their money in a drug deal with the Mafioso. At the same time, they reportedly set up a car bomb, which fortunately did not kill anyone. They kept making attempts to hide behind us, and even resorted to threats, as they planned their dastardly deeds, but the Lord thwarted them at every turn. It did not take very long before Walter, Carrillo, and the Mafioso were all in jail in a maximum security penitentiary serving very long sentences. Even from jail, Walter attempted to blackmail me, but it eventually came to nothing. We continue to pray for him. Nevertheless, this and other situations made for some very trying moments because in Colombia you are guilty until proven innocent, and there is no bail.

By this time, there were so many wonderful officers all over the country dedicated to the Lord that we were finding friends everywhere.

# CHAPTER 9

# The Least Shall Be the Greatest

A black bus driver in the northern peninsula of the Guajira, named Jacobo Gomez, had a dream in which the Lord told him he was going to be a senator of The Republic. Jubilant, he went and told his pastor. The pastor frowned and tried to pour cold water on the idea. In Spanish *Senator* is *Senador* and *janitor* is *Celador* (pronounced Selador). "I think you heard wrong," the pastor chided, "I think the Lord probably said that you were going to be a janitor."

Jacobo, however, was not to be deterred. He joined a political party and started to work his way up the ladder. Colombian elections allow every candidate to post the names of their second, third, fourth, and so on persons on the totem pole, and they combine their votes in a national election for senators. If the combined votes are enough, they may get the top guy elected, or if they are really lucky, the top two or three names may all get elected. If something happens to the first guy, then everyone else moves up the ladder.

The black guy (number five on the list) only got about three thousand votes, but his team got enough to elect the top candidate. Soon, however, the Supreme Court put that guy in jail for alleged unauthorized meetings with paramilitary groups. The next guy had health problems, somebody else passed away, and before you knew it, Jacobo Gomez was the senator.

A wonderful Christian friend of ours named Jorge Castellanos took the fledgling senator under his wing. Jorge is a top lawyer and also an excellent journalist who has held a number of first class positions. After a few months, his protégé got the idea that he wanted to find a top notch Christian politician from the United States and honor him in the Colombian Senate. He was put in contact with Marco Rubio, who at the time was still in the Florida State Legislature.

Out of the blue, I got a beautiful white invitation embossed with gold from the senator inviting Mr. and Mrs. Russell Martin Stendal to the elaborate ceremony where Marco Rubio would receive the highest honors at the Senate rotunda. Unfortunately, I was already double booked. I had to meet with a small-town mayor about a very critical situation, and the meeting could not be put off.

Suddenly, I had an inspiration. My son, Russell Martin Stendal Jr., has my same name. He was seventeen years old. I called him in and handed him the invitation telling him to dress up in his best clothes and take his sister Alethia with him. After all, it said Mr. and Mrs. Russell Martin Stendal. I told them to identify themselves to security at the entrance with their US passports and went off with Marina to meet with the mayor halfway across the country.

When the security agents at the Colombian Senate saw Russell Jr. and Alethia in the line with their US passports in their hands and dressed fit to kill, they pulled them out of the line and took them directly to the senator. They spent the rest of the afternoon with the black Christian senator and with Marco Rubio, who became very interested in our ministry. Russell Jr. gave him copies of our books and came back with a card from Marco addressed to me and with his offer to be of service in any way. Senator Jacobo Gomez told then Florida State Representative, Marco Rubio, that he felt that God wanted

Marco to become a United States Senator and to become seriously involved in US national politics. He went home with the blessing and with the highest honors of the Colombian Senate. The rest is history.

I had a fruitful meeting with the mayor and continued on to Cali and then to Popayan. General Barrero had been named commander of the 29th Brigade in Popayan. He had made a major discovery that would change the course of the war in Southwest Colombia. He started asking captured prisoners and deserters if there were any factors or unique circumstances that made it difficult for terrorists or illegal armed groups to operate and prosper. They all replied that yes, wherever evangelical Christians dominate society back in the labyrinths of endless mountain ranges, deep valleys, and trackless river deltas pouring to the Pacific Ocean, none of the violent groups are able to prosper. The Christians refuse to participate in illegal activity.

So General Barrero, a Roman Catholic, got the bright idea of helping promote evangelical Christianity with all the resources at his command. The entire Department (State) was in such desperate shape that soon the Catholic Governor of Cauca was also on board. I was given special permission to set up a network of Christian non-sectarian radio stations. We flooded the entire area with hundreds of thousands of books, Bibles, and other materials. The general started a Christian Indians association with 3,500 leaders. Ray Rising and I were invited to the first meeting.

Among the Paez or Naza Indians, starting with Canadian missionaries back in 1932, God has lit a fire. Wycliffe Bible Translators Mariana Slocum and Florence Girdel did an excellent translation of the Paez New Testament back in the 1970s. Tom and Karen Branks did a wonderful job with the Guambiano Indians. My dad, who coordinated the Wycliffe

Bible translation work in Colombia until 1974, thinks these two teams are among the best Bible translators ever.

Now the general began to fan the blaze of what God was doing, and things went into overdrive. It gradually became apparent to me that there were tens of thousands of Christian Indians out there, multiplying like rabbits in the midst of some of the worst persecution we have ever seen or heard tell of.

Soon the forces of evil retaliated. Dark interests got the general transferred. His new command was the 6th Division in Florencia, Caqueta. News was out, however, that General Leonardo Barrero was a straight shooter. Dozens, even hundreds of guerrillas and paramilitaries, began to surrender to him as God continued to bless him. After a year and a half, he was sent back to Cali as commander of the 3rd Division. He moved the Division Headquarters from Cali to Popayan to be as far as possible from corrupt politics and as close as possible to the war zone. One of his first orders was to call me and ask me to restore the radio stations, which for the most part had dwindled or been shut down in his absence.

I started having problems in eastern Colombia. One night at Lomalinda, one of our neighbors came over late and breathlessly told me that there were twenty heavily armed guerrillas on the other side of the lake trying to decide whether or not to surrender to the paramilitary or to the Colombian Army. They were requesting that I meet with them urgently. Someone was waiting down at the edge of the lake with a canoe to take me over to the other side. I must come quickly. They were hungry, and our over-eager neighbor claimed he had just sent them nine roast chickens, and they had eaten everything. I began to smell a rat.

I called the commanding Army colonel for the area. He was able to send a rapid response team immediately to my aid with two men on a motorcycle that arrived almost immediately.

Instead of twenty guerrilla deserters, four common criminals were down at the edge of the lake a couple hundred yards from our house, in what was most likely an attempt to kidnap me. Two were captured the next day and put in jail. I began to receive death threats.

Things deteriorated from bad to worse as bands of common criminals were wandering to and fro, hiring out to the highest bidder. Most of the cocaine fields for a hundred miles around Lomalinda had been sprayed with herbicide by the government. The chemical had not only killed the drug fields, but it also got most of the gardens and even some of the pastures. The people who were used to easy money from the drug trade became more and more desperate. Cattle rustling and kidnapping increased dramatically.

They would put surveillance teams in the jungle near our installations and wait for weeks for me to show up. Once I came in with Ray Rising, Wayne Borthwick, and others. We spent several days installing complex, shortwave antennas to boost the signal of our 6010 kHz signal on the 49-meter band named *La Voz de Tu Conscience* (*The Voice of Your Conscience*). We were able to finish our work a couple of days earlier than we had planned and I had announced, so one night we left for Bogotá. By this time the unarmed surveillance team had finally figured out we were there. We drove off while their friends were rushing to their aid with the weapons. Later, a bar owner we knew told us about the guys that came in the next night and got drunk, lamenting about the gringos in the red truck (me and my friends) that got away.

Another time, I was out at the Lomalinda radio station, tuning the equipment and making trips back into the remote jungle to Eduardo's area and behind the Macarena Mountains, when I got a kidney stone. In remote eastern Colombia, there is no option of calling 911. Plus, the FAA had expressed concern about my past history in this area. They told me that if I had one more reported incident of being hospitalized for a kidney stone, my medical would be reevaluated. I had a few minutes warning as I felt major trouble coming on. I took some medicine I had on hand to relax my body in the hope that I could pass the stone. As the pain increased and I paced back and forth, I did not relish the idea of having one of my guys drive me over the terrible washboard roads to the nearest hospital. Finally, I found a six pack of beer – having been told by my doctor that this would dilate my urethra, serve as a disinfectant, and prevent infection in the internal lacerations the kidney stone would cause as it came down my urinary tract.

I found myself praying and drinking beer and counting the minutes. Five minutes was an eternity. Then I would brace myself and try to make it through another five minutes. I could not lie down. I was extremely miserable and exhausted standing up. Each time I thought I was at the maximum pain threshold that I could endure, it would continue to ratchet up and get worse. As in other difficult situations, the Lord's voice came in loud and clear the entire time. He kept giving me insight on many situations and instructions of what should be our next moves. Before I could finish the six pack, I suddenly passed the stone and immediately came into perfect peace. To call this a stone is a bit of a misnomer. It looked like a cocklebur made out of razor sharp glass.

After that, I survived two assassination attempts plus endured trouble from corrupt individuals, including Walter, who were attempting to blackmail me by threatening to give false testimony against me and get me thrown in jail. In the midst of all this, many on all sides were turning to the Lord and yearning for freedom from the tangled web that had been their lives. Driving through the drug fields deep in the jungle, men and women would flag me down and tell me how important our radio broadcasts were to them. One drug grower proudly told me they were such faithful listeners to our Lomalinda radio station that they did not even switch channels when the preaching came on.

If I pulled into a general store or got on a riverboat or a bus, they would most likely be tuned in to one of our stations. I found places where Christian church buildings and meetings were still strictly prohibited, yet it seemed that at least half of the people were converted. Their vocabulary had changed; their habits had changed; they no longer lived in conflict with their families and with their neighbors. Some of the ones who had been causing the most trouble now became peacemakers with a powerful ministry for the Lord.

I began to analyze the testimonies. Many of them had never been in a church building or even in a home meeting. They had never even heard of raising their hand when no one is looking to respond to an invitation. They had no idea what an altar call was or what a sinner's prayer was. Our radio programs preaching through the Bible stick exactly to the Bible, and we found no examples of Jesus or the apostles doing any of the aforementioned. Yet most of the Colombian people know more about the Scriptures than someone who has been to Bible school or seminary for many years. They listened to hours and hours of me preaching through the Bible every day, and this went on for years.

Then one day it dawned on me. Jesus sent forth his disciples and said that if someone received them, it was the same as receiving the Lord, and if they received him, they also received his Father who sent him. Jesus said that if someone receives a righteous man because he is a righteous man, they will receive the reward of a righteous man. The reward of a righteous man is eternal life (Matthew 25:46). Jesus said that if someone receives a prophet because he is a prophet, they will receive the reward of a prophet. Who is a prophet? Someone who speaks words from God instead of his own words (Matthew 10:39-42).

## Matthew 9

> 38 *pray ye therefore the Lord of the harvest, that he will send forth labourers into his harvest.*

The Lord sends workers, and if they are received, then He is received. This is his method of evangelism and boy does it ever work!

The workers, however, must really have been sent by the Lord. In order for this to happen, they have to have a direct encounter with him. The presence of the Lord cripples the natural man. Jacob had a direct encounter with God and limped for the rest of his life. But his name (nature) had been changed from Jacob (conniver) to Israel (Prince with God). Those who have been directly in the presence of God are marked. They are broken. They no longer care about any of the things or affairs of this world. They only live – counting the remaining days of their prison sentence here on earth – to do his will and to make him happy. They yearn to permanently be in his presence.

## Mark 9

> 34 *But they* [the disciples] *were silent; for on the way they had disputed among themselves, who should be the greatest.*
>
> 35 *Then, sitting down, he called the twelve and said unto them, If anyone desires to be first, the same shall be last of all and servant of all.*
>
> 36 *And taking a child, he set him in the midst of them; and taking him in his arms, he said unto them,*

*37 Whosoever shall receive one of such children in my name, receives me; and whosoever shall receive me, receives not me, but him that sent me.*

All of these people with changed lives and with changed appetites had been receiving me and my coworkers whom God had been sending out into the harvest fields with me. This is how the Lord got his foot in the door and how he came into their hearts (John 13:20). Last year we deployed close to 200,000 parachutes, and almost every one had an item for the children (for some their first toy is the parachute). A huge number of children have seen the movie, and many spontaneously respond with a strong desire to commit their lives to God to be a missionary like me. He loves to use children!

## Luke 9

*46 Then there rose a dispute among them, which of them should be greatest.*

*47 But Jesus, seeing the thoughts of their heart, took a child and set him by him,*

*48 and said unto them, Whosoever shall receive this child in my name receives me, and whosoever shall receive me receives him that sent me; for he that is least among you all, the same shall be great.*

The most unexpected result when the movie *La Montana* is shown happens with pastors. We expected to reach guerrillas, paramilitary, soldiers, and campesino farmers. The salty language in the film gives authenticity to rough characters in their natural state. We thought most churches and pastors would not want to show the PG-13 film. Boy were we ever wrong! One eight-year-old girl came up to Lisa after seeing the movie and exclaimed, "Now I know that only bad people use that kind of language."

The pastors, however, have been the group most affected by the movie. Many cannot even talk for a long time. They come under very intense conviction because they have been within the four walls of their church fortresses fighting over sheep, over money, over doctrine ... and they have not been out in the highways and byways, compelling the lost to come in. They have not been allowing the Lord to use them as the bait on the hook to fish for lost souls. Many pastors have been so convicted that they know the Lord is telling them to bring their entire ministries to a screeching halt and start over God's way.

# CHAPTER 10

# When God Likes Something, He Multiplies It

V OM Finland sent us an offering to publish material for children to put in our parachutes. About this same time, Steve Linquist, from VOM USA had sent us the finished artwork and Spanish translation of the *Kids for Courage* children's books written by Cheryl Odden. The first one is called *God's Bandit* and is the story of William Tyndale and the English Bible. We thought the offering would be enough to print 10,000 of the beautiful books, but we were in for a big surprise when we got to the Buena Semilla print shop. Juan Muñoz, the general manager, said that it was the best book that had ever come through his office. He took the offering from the Finlanders and made us 30,000 of the books. Then we went on through the year printing the rest of the *Kids for Courage* series as more and more help arrived.

Disaster struck again, and General Barrero was replaced at the 3rd Division and given a desk job at Military Headquarters in Bogotá. We began to wonder if we would be able to keep the radio stations in Valle and Cauca on the air. Things began to appear very shaky as some of the new military commanders were like the Pharaoh in the Bible who did not know Joseph.

Then the Naza Indians went on the rampage. They closed

down the Pan America highway many times and in many places. They even marched on Bogotá. Thousands of Nazas, armed with their characteristic staffs, attacked and overran police and Army posts. The poor policemen and soldiers were afraid to shoot the irate Indians who did not have firearms. So the Nazas overran the government positions, captured dozens, even hundreds of policemen and soldiers and destroyed their weapons.

The president of Colombia decided to go out and talk with them face to face. After all, he had done this several times with meetings lined up with General Barrero. The Naza are very fierce and tenacious. Without the Lord, they are hard to deal with. The Pilgrims had not landed in Colombia. The Spanish Conquistadores had, followed by the Spanish Inquisition. After that, they had to deal with bandits, guerrillas, paramilitary forces and drug traffickers. The only good outsiders had been a few, fleeting glimpses of foreign missionaries. General Barrero had lined up the president with meetings with Naza leaders but had flanked the area with Christian Nazas (there are now reported to be more than 80,000 of them). These Nazas are fierce and tenacious for the Lord. They do not give up even when tortured unmercifully for their faith. Even if their church buildings and homes are destroyed, they continue to send teams of evangelists back into the tribal areas where they were displaced. Even the little children are soundly converted and on fire for the Lord.

President Santos walked right into a trap. Thousands of upset Nazas began to beat up his security forces. Guerrillas took advantage of the disorder and set up their roadblocks on all the roads leading in and out of the site chosen for the presidential meeting. The president's security advisers panicked and called in fighter planes to make low passes over the crowd in a show of force. The guerrillas approached to within one thousand meters of the president. News crews and cameras were everywhere.

The Naza started pushing dozens of policemen over the side of an inclined cliff, many of whom are still quadriplegic or in wheelchairs now. One of the fighters crashed in front of the news cameras. The guerrillas claimed they had shot it down. The government claims it was an accident. President Santos was very fortunate to get extricated out of such a big mess and back to his office in Bogotá.

He fired the new military commander of SW Colombia. Under military protocol, in order to be able to return General Barrero to the area, he had to create a new task force including Army, Navy, and Air Force for Barrero to command. This was because Barrero had technically been passed over for promotion and the new Army commander was junior to him. Therefore Barrero was given this new command under the Colombian equivalent of the Joint Chiefs of Staff. He accepted with one condition. He got the president to allow him to pick a dream team of all the best officers, noncoms, and enlisted men in all the Armed Forces from all over the country.

The move of God had spread like wildfire into the Armed Forces, and when Barrero concentrated the best people into his Southwest Pacific Task Force, it hit critical mass. All of a sudden, we were dealing with hundreds and then thousands of leaders (they do not like to use the term pastor because so many pastors have been killed by terrorists). Barrero's people began to pick projects for us, and we put in radio stations for the Christian Naza and Guambianos. We were asked to help Naza refugees. VOM Finland, encouraged by what had happened with their offering for children's materials, came to Colombia and Johani, Aki, and Loki fell in love with a group of fifty Naza families that had been displaced by a combination of persecution and a volcano that blew up and destroyed their village. They had been living in dire conditions for seven years – sleeping on the ground on plastic with no decent water or sanitary facilities on less than an acre of rented land where they were not allowed to build any permanent structure.

When we asked them what they needed, their leader, Marco Tulio, replied "We are alive, we also have our Christian school-teachers and our pastors. We are concerned for the Christians up in the mountains who are suffering terribly. Most of them do not even have Bibles. Please give us Bibles for outreach." The Finns purchased land for a new village which the Naza rebuilt in record time. God began to send in specialists from all over. The Naza soon named their new village The Greatness of God. My son-in-law, Samuel Hernandez, and my daughter, Lisa, have worked tirelessly for a long time to coordinate this project and many others all across this nation.

Jean and Sandy Bergeron brought a group of Canadians down to encourage the Naza. They brought wool and yarn and taught classes to the women on how to sew and knit and crochet. One day, the Canadian ladies noticed that some of the Naza ladies were doing a beautiful stitch that they had never seen before. They asked the Naza where they had learned this. A Naza lady replied, "In the 1930s some Canadian missionaries came to our village and taught this to my grandparents."

It was only after the Canadian ladies spent a couple of weeks making friends with the Naza that they opened up and began to share the truth about the horrible persecution they had been suffering, many times at the hands of their own people. The Naza were greatly encouraged by the Canadians and vice versa.

Greg Musselman of VOM Canada came down and did an excellent video about this. I was interpreting when he interviewed the wife of a key Naza leader (pastor) who had been through quite a lot, and her family had scars to prove it. Greg asked if, now that she was a Christian, it was a great comfort to know that when she died she would go to heaven. She replied that she knew she would go to heaven but that was not foremost on her mind. She said, "You see, we no longer serve those little gods of our ancestors. Now we serve the big God. We keep going back up into those mountains and our big God is going to deliver those people who persecuted us into our hands. They are also going to come to know our big God. This is what we live for! We will not rest until they are all saved and converted by our big God."

The Naza Indians were some of the founders of the guerrilla movement fifty years ago. Now, what God is doing among them is literally enough to take your breath away. It is not easy to make friends with them, but once they are your friends, they will never turn on you. They will always put friendship above any other factor except God. They seem to naturally and perfectly understand the ways of God. They instinctively understand that those that are led by the Spirit of God are not under the law (Romans 6:14; Galatians 5:18). They blatantly go against the tribal laws and even the laws of Colombia as the Spirit leads them. Once a Christian radio station is in their hands and on their land, they will not let anyone shut it down. The Guambianos are the same.

Christian radio beams from the tribal highlands and now hits the big cities on the plains and valleys far below. Millions of people are in range of their broadcasts. Taxi drivers cannot believe their ears. The unstoppable Indians, feared by the city dwellers because at the drop of a hat they can shut down all the roads into Cali and elsewhere, are now talking about God with great conviction. The messages and testimonies are unbelievable.

I was due to show the movie last year on Good Friday to an event planned by an Army colonel on the way to Ecuador. At the last minute, he was given leave and decided to cancel the event. I decided to meander up into the mountains and explore some places I had been warned not to go. After following some roads back into the high mountains, I walked up a high ridge at about 11,000 feet that had electric lines. There was a little radio station at the top that was on the air with 67 watts of power. The local Guambiano pastor, who was also the vice governor of the entire tribe, was up there with his leaders praying that God would send them help to beef up their little radio station. I walked into the prayer meeting and was immediately taken as the answer to their prayers.

After we beefed up the transmitter, it was only a matter of time before the police arrived to shut the thing down. The Guambianos were cordial but firm. We were here first, and you white men came here last. This is our land. We will not allow you to arrest us; but how about if we arrest you? They served a nice lunch to the policemen who warily eyed the hundreds of Guambianos who had begun to gather. After lunch the police left and never came back. Their treaty says that the Indians can do what they want on their own land. The little church had been under constant persecution from 1932 to 2012 (eighty years), and then many of the tribal leaders became Christians and Christians were put into power. Now they are beginning to face a different type of trial. It is called prosperity. Churches in North America have been almost completely devastated by this scourge. Back in Bible times the children of Israel did not seem to do so well under prosperity either.

A veteran who served in Afghanistan and was living in Fairbanks, Alaska, with his family felt led to sell his Harley Davidson motorcycle and buy a ticket to Colombia. A few days later, I showed up in Fairbanks to speak at a VOM conference. There were tears in his eyes when I invited him to come to Cauca and help the Paez. Jon Dufendach came and installed a big water purification system with enough pure water for over 10,000 people because the Naza wanted to hold a huge event on the new property. They built a big warehouse and began to pray God would fill it with Bibles. Now it is filled with graphic, full-color booklets about the teachings of Jesus since the David C. Cook ministry donated 3.5 million of them at the suggestion and coordination of Reed Olson and Mike King. Children are now being mobilized to use these booklets as invitations to invite their friends to see our movie or to come to a Christian event or church.

Other key visitors who have been of great assistance to the persecuted believers are Jim Dau, David Witt, and Mark and Cindy Millar. Daniel Hernandez, Jony, and Jonathan are also working on ideas to help support the thousands of leaders who are under fire in the midst of strong persecution, but also standing strong in the midst of one of the most interesting and fruitful moves of God that I have ever seen. Albert Luepnitz has been on several trips with me and Alethia into Naza and Guambiano territory, and we have witnessed many miracles.

Dan Janzen, an agricultural expert from Michigan, was on his way to the Sudan in Africa when rebels took over the village in which he was going to work. He emailed me and shifted his ticket to Colombia. Now the Naza are cultivating all kinds of wonderful and even exotic fruit and vegetables that no one in the area has ever seen before, and that is helping them to feed their families and reach out to their enemies. No one, including myself, has ever seen such wonderful and consistent fruit of the Spirit.

When the non-Christians in the area gather to riot, protest, and shut down the highways, the Christians plan big rallies in the covered arenas that were built all over the middle of nowhere in years past by a political boondoggle. Almost everyone can recognize my old 1988 Toyota from the movie, so they let us through even when everyone else is having trouble.

One day Luis Humberto Montejo and I flew into Cali on a special trip to see General Barrero to ask his help and advice on how to respond to an initiative from Noel, the guerrilla commander featured in the movie. Noel is also a Naza Indian, which makes the movie a very hot topic that even the non-Christian Nazas love to watch. After we met with the general, who promised to help coordinate our activities with the government, we were sent to the airport in the general's new truck. In the middle of a major thoroughfare, the left rear wheel came off and also caused the brakes to malfunction. The tire went careening ahead of us and into a stream that flowed into a canal through the city. We were unharmed and another vehicle was sent to rescue us. If the general had been in the vehicle, the driver would have been going much faster. In fact, the whole thing could have been an attempt to harm the general.

A few months later, General Barrero was unexpectedly named the supreme military commander for all the Colombian Armed Forces. From day one, all different types of obscure and dark forces attempted to unseat him. Somehow he managed to last six months before he was forced to resign. During those six months, however, he attempted to apply his policies, which had been so successful on a national scale in Southwest Colombia. He appointed excellent officers to many key posts. He opened many more doors for our ministry. Now retired from active military duty, I am sure that he will be even more effective for the Lord.

God has raised up many other excellent active duty officers to take his place. Just to name a few: General Nestor Robinson (the Colonel in the movie). General Juan Pablo Amaya (now the Southeast Task Force Commander) has given us the same warm welcome that General Barrero gave us at his task force. General Jorge Segura, the 3rd Division Commander under Barrero who was so helpful to us is now head of all of Colombian Army Aviation. Time and space will not allow me to list the thousands of people on all sides of this conflict who have embraced us, and somehow God has gained a great foothold in their hearts and lives, which spreads to others.

Up in a remote mountain overlooking the Cauca Valley, a guerrilla unit thought they were doing society a favor when they shot and killed a local brujo or spiritualist (a local shaman) who had allegedly done some nefarious deeds. However, the man turned out to be a Naza Indian. This killing caused the local tribal leaders to become very incensed. They captured the first five FARC guerrilla militia that they could lay their hands on – including an eighteen-year-old boy – and beat the tar out of them with their staffs. They put them on trial, and sentenced them to forty years each in prison with no appeal and no parole, as the Colombian government has a treaty obligation to put anyone sentenced by the Indians into the government penitentiary. At the trial, the communists tried to marshal a popular protest, but the Indians beat up hundreds of communists. I saw little old ladies with triple purple and blue bruises on their heads – one bruise on top of another – when Dr. Fernando and I went up to be of help.

All of a sudden, I started getting calls from guerrillas asking me to help them calm down the Nazas. A number of guerrilla militia now desired to be identified as Christians instead of communists, so they were asking for boxes of Bibles and copies of our movie for their own use and to pass out among the furious Nazas in an attempt to moderate their image.

There are now Naza and Guambiano evangelists traveling all over. Men like Ever and Henry and countless others are standing for the truth. Some have been put in the stocks and torture machines that the Paez and other tribes have copied from the Spanish Inquisition (machines that literally tear the person limb from limb). Others have been killed or they disappeared in the midst of the armed conflict. Many have lost their church buildings, their homes, or even their loved ones.

Many military officers have been apparently fired for the cause of the gospel. Countless guerrillas, militia, paramilitary, policemen, and soldiers have had to choose between following orders and taking a stand for the Lord.

We are proud to serve the Lord in the midst of this conflict. Our young people have caught fire for God above and beyond our wildest dreams. When I was recently asked in the United States if I have any contingency plans to be implemented in the event that someone kills me, I replied that everything is in compartments and each compartment has a God-appointed leader with full authority and responsibility to respond instantly to any crisis. Yet each one is also surrounded by a team of associates that will back them up. Because of all the wonderful and unique ongoing friendships that God has given me over the years, I used to say the only thing I can do that no one else can do is to be a personal liaison with top leaders. Now, I dare say that even in this area, I am about to be eclipsed by my children, by my associates, and by so many young people who are fearlessly following the call of God.

# Part II

The Account Written
by Alethia Stendal

# Introduction

When a friend of mine read this manuscript, he said, "The stories of the people in this book are so personal. You might offend them if you write them all into a book."

I thought about it for a few seconds and replied, "It stopped being their own personal story the moment their decisions affected the lives of every human being in this country. The families of all of the countless victims in Colombia deserve to know what was really developing on the island."

What happens around us may seem dark and discouraging at times, but we can rest assured there will always be hope as long as there is at least one bended knee. The only thing for which God truly searches in order to respond to our cries, is for hearts that are willing to lay down their lives for their brothers, as Judah, Daniel, and our Lord Jesus Christ did.

# CHAPTER 11

# Eyes Shut Tight

*May 2010*

My whole life, my mom, grandma, and others criticized me for slouching. I thought I had a bad habit until six months ago when my dad invited me to join him and take pictures of an ex-officers' breakfast meeting at a military base. Well, he didn't actually invite me; I sort of just got in the car with him. On the way, the engine broke down, and our old Toyota wouldn't start again. In a big hurry to get to the meeting, my dad wanted me to wait for the tow truck. But being a bit of a persistent person, I insisted that he not leave me because I really wanted to go with him. So we turned the key a few more times. On about the fifth try, my dad said, "If it doesn't work this time, you have to stay, 'cause I can't miss this meeting." He put the key in the ignition; I said a quick prayer, and the engine started.

When we arrived at the breakfast, there were two tables of former generals and colonels who had been thrown into jail for allegedly violating human rights during their service. One by one they stood and complained about how unjustly they had been treated. Then an older American man named Albert Luepnitz spoke of how in 2005 the Lord had told him to tell President Álvaro Uribe Vélez he would be re-elected and to start forming intercessory groups to pray for the peace of Colombia. Albert tried thinking of ways to contact the president, but finally he came to this conclusion: "Lord, if this is really something you want, then have the president call me."

The next morning, Albert received a phone call from the president himself asking for a private meeting. In this meeting, Albert told President Uribe he was going to get re-elected and the Lord was going to give him wisdom on how to deal with his enemies. President Uribe said this was impossible because the constitution would not allow that to happen. However, Albert responded that the Lord had spoken and even if the constitution had to be changed, it would happen.

During his talk, Albert told of all the healings he had witnessed in Colombia, especially in the army. He told incredible stories of deaf and blind soldiers being healed and twisted limbs straightening out. My dad translated, and in the meantime I was busy taking pictures when out of nowhere after the meeting had ended, Albert came up to me and said, "Do you have a back problem?"

I thought, "I hope he didn't notice my slouch. How embarrassing." My first reply was, "No, not that I can think of." But then I remembered all of the things my mom would say about standing up straight. So I said he could pray for me if he wanted.

Albert sat me on a chair with my back centered and measured my two legs. To my surprise, one was longer than the other by about an inch. Albert said, "You see, you have one leg shorter than the other one?"

I said, "Yes."

Then he said, "We're going to ask the Lord Jesus to make it even with the other one."

In a moment of panic I thought, "Oh, poor old man. He's going to pray, and nothing's going to happen, and then I'm going to have to pretend that I'm all better." Yes, all those thoughts can run through your mind in a matter of seconds, but he prayed for me while I had my eyes shut tight. After seeing many more miracles in my life, I realize you should never close your eyes because God might do something, and you just might miss it.

My leg grew to the size of the other one, and although I didn't see it because I had my eyes closed, it made a huge difference for me ever since. And then Albert had me stand up, and he checked my back and saw that my spine was crooked. He said, "You feel this here? It's twisted." As he was praying, I felt as if a gentle hand had softly straightened it, like when you straighten out your fingers after clenching them in a fist. I walked out of that breakfast meeting feeling like a completely new person.

I felt as though I had never danced before or played soccer or slept well or even walked straight. A load was taken off my back, and I needed to leap out of there and try again all the things I had once loved to do. I learned that no matter how crooked you are, it is impossible to straighten yourself out. The only one who can straighten you out is God, both spiritually and physically, but you are the one who gives the consent. And sometimes (like in my case), you don't even know that you need straightening, but when you get straight, you feel a huge difference.

I traveled to Canada and the United States and spoke at some places about what God was doing in Colombia with the radio stations, the books, and Bibles. When I came back, I discovered I had a new roommate. Her name was Joanna, and she belonged to the FARC guerrilla movement. Her commander was the top guerrilla leader at that time. Our suspicion was that they sent her to spy on us under the pretext that she was sick. When she got here, it turned out she really was sick.

We took her to several different doctors. They ran tests and found out her spinal cord was severely deteriorated, and the muscles in her back were damaged. The doctors determined they could not fix her problem. The only thing they could do was to teach her to do therapy for her back, but they said that no matter what she did, she would be in pain for the rest of her life. Joanna was devastated when she heard this. She had been sick for twelve years. That day I tried my best to console her as she cried in bitter pain near my bed. She started going to muscle therapy twice a week and learned well. Nevertheless, every night she would complain about how everything hurt.

Joanna stayed with us for three months, and during that time, her heart softened. One day, I found her crying in the living room. When I asked her what was wrong, she told me that she missed her mom. I wasn't expecting that answer to come from a tough guerrilla girl. So I told her we would make arrangements for her to see her mom, and a week later her mom and grandmother came to visit. She had not seen them since she ran away from home fourteen years before. They had been praying for her ever since. Sadly, her mom was killed only a few weeks after the reunion.

One day, as we were walking into a movie theatre, she told my mom and me that the way we talked about God was admirable. She said we talked about Him as if we really knew Him, and she wanted to know Him too. Joanna's heart was beginning to change. Of all the guests we'd ever had from Colombia and elsewhere, by far she had the most hungering docile heart and longing for God.

A few days before she left for the jungle, my dad called me in the room and told me Albert was here again, and he asked me what I thought of taking Joanna to see him. My mom and I talked with her in the living room, and I told her how the Lord had healed me, and if she had even a little faith, He could do it for her too. I gave her the option of going or staying. She listened intently and decided to go. We didn't tell her, however, that this man was waiting for us on a military base. My sister Lisa, my mom, my dad, Joanna, and I drove down to the base. She told us later that when she realized where we were taking her, she almost had a heart attack. After all, these were the people she had fought against all her life. We saw armed and camouflaged military personnel everywhere. It was all I could do to contain my laughter as I imagined what was going on in her mind.

We walked into the private dining room in the ornate officers' club where Albert was, and he prayed for her. She had the same problem I had where one leg was shorter than the other, and we all saw it healed. And then she stood up, and Albert prayed for her back, and the hump and dents that were there were completely straightened. She said afterward that she felt a hot tingling come over her whole body. She felt no pain from that point on.

As we walked out, she told me she was glad she had her own experience with God because now she knew for sure that He existed and He loved her. This happened on April 12, 2010, exactly six months after I was healed. To me this was significant because I realized God didn't show favoritism, no matter who the people were or what they had done. Joanna went back to the guerrillas a few days later. Her last words to Lisa and me as she left were that she couldn't leave the FARC movement because they might kill her or someone she loved, but now she couldn't behave as badly as she had before. She asked us to pray for her freedom.

Albert came to our meeting to record a message for our radio stations that transmit in the war-torn areas of Colombia where people are really hungry for the gospel. People are free to come and listen to the recording session if they want. This is done so the preachers have an audience and the messages come out better. God again did marvelous things through him. One little girl couldn't talk since she had seen someone murder her father years ago. Albert sat her on his lap and began to sing

"Jesus Loves Me" to her. My brother translated the words, and soon she began to sing back, and then she was able to talk!

The most important thing for everybody was to realize that the Lord was the one who was healing, and nobody but Him got the credit. My mom told me that she learned when you walk with the Lord, He gives you so much love, and the love of God will bring healing to the nations, whether it is physical healing or spiritual healing.

Albert Luepnitz is eighty-five years old and retired from the US Army. He has been coming to Colombia at his own expense every year for the past thirty years to pray for wounded and sick soldiers and guerrillas. He began as a Full Gospel Businessman setting up meetings all over South America. But one day, when he returned to North America, the Lord showed him a vision of him preaching, and from the pulpit he saw that it was a crowd of Latin American people. The Lord told him that was where he needed to be ministering. When he returned to Colombia and spoke for the very first time, he saw that same exact vision in real life, and he has been coming down here ever since.

The day after Joanna went back to the guerrillas (April 19), we were worried that government bombers would bomb her camp. We got the following email:

> Sonrise in Whitehorse received your prayer alert, and as I was praying for your people in Colombia and other places in South America, I saw the following vision:

> I saw bomber planes flying overhead. They were flying over campfires where natives were dancing around the fires doing a war dance. Then I saw white sheets cover some campfire scenes. The sheets represented the people totally surrendering to God. At some campfires, there were no white sheets

*because those people were unable to surrender. The
places that were surrendered were safe from the
bomber planes; the planes simply looked and flew
on by them. The places that did not surrender left
themselves open for attacks from the planes.*

When Joanna left, my dad told her to tell her commander, Jorge, that God was giving him one last chance to turn to Him. If he didn't, he would most likely die. This was one of the most obstinate guerrilla commanders that had caused much damage and persecution (he reportedly ordered more than 400 pastors killed), but God was giving him one last chance to repent.

Months went by and we never heard back from Joanna. Finally, we received a report stating Commander Jorge's camp had been bombed, and everyone had died. An intelligence army colonel told my dad they had found Jorge's computer, and one of the last orders he wrote was: "Capture the gringo," meaning my dad. He was bombed before he had a chance to send the order out. They told us Joanna had died too.

I was sad, but something in my heart didn't believe it. I couldn't believe God would have so many special dealings with her and then she would be bombed and killed a few months later. Besides, she had repented. Weren't the sheets seen in the vision supposed to have covered the people who surrendered to God?

A year went by and still we didn't hear anything. Lisa and I began to film a script we had written, a true story of how God brought peace to one of the most dangerous, war-inflicted mountains in the country. Our movie, called *La Montaña* (meaning "The Mountain"), came out, and we still saw no sign of Joanna. However, one day she appeared at one of our premieres. Seeing her was like seeing a dead person come to life again. Everyone gave her a nice, warm welcome. And one of my friends, who didn't know she was a guerrilla, gave her a special thick, heavy, waterproof Bible. To my friend's complete astonishment, Joanna tore the heavy Bible in half and said to her guerrilla friend, "Here, stick half of it in your pack, and I'll carry the other half. That will make it easier to carry in the jungle."

We were happy that she was impressed with the movie because one of the main characters is Noel (a FARC guerrilla commander), someone she knew very well because he had been her leader. She exclaimed, "You guys got him down perfectly! Every gesture is exactly like Camarada Noel."

# CHAPTER 12

# Noel's Invitation

In November 2012, we continued showing the movie in all parts of the country. Never could we have imagined how everyone would relate to the story in such a personal way or how it would awaken a feeling hidden deep inside every Colombian's heart – a longing for our country to finally find peace. Real peace. But that wasn't the reality of our situation. Peace negotiations between the FARC and the Colombian government had begun a month before in Oslo, Norway. Most of the country felt, because of previous supposed peace plans, it was just another big political scam to further perpetrate a darker purpose.

This war goes back too far, and everyone has deep hurts that are impossible to heal without God's divine intervention. I watched the number one FARC negotiator, Ivan Márquez, on live TV, giving what seemed like a Castro-Chavez-Marxist political campaign speech. My whole body cringed. I thought to myself, "Is this really how things are going to end? A communist takeover and that's it?" I got on my knees and prayed, and I think many others who love this country also prayed that day.

A friend told me as I was ranting to him about the peace negotiations now taking place in Cuba, "Be assured, Alethia, terrorism will not reign as long as there is at least one bended knee."

Noel was one of my dad's former enemies who had kid-napped him years before, but by God's mercy, they had become very good friends for the past thirty years. They formed what they call *"Plan Amigos"* which is a sort of "Friend's Plan," ini-tiated by Noel himself in an effort to solve the war. In Noel's own words, it basically means, "your friends can become my friends, and my friends can become your friends as long as all of us are willing to take a stand against corruption." So if my dad has a friend who is a soldier or a paramilitary, he can also be a friend with Noel who is a guerrilla. Therefore, a huge gap between two conflicting sides is easily bridged. It really is a simple solution.

Albert Einstein said, "When the solution is simple, God is answering." And I believe him. For years now, my dad and Noel have been practicing this Plan Amigos.

They had so many good stories of what happened as a result that it inspired my sister Lisa and me to write some of them down and eventually make them into the full feature movie *La Montaña*. My dad had not heard from Noel in more than a year, but one day we received a clandestine message from Havana, Cuba. It was from Noel, the same Noel from the movie. Apparently he had become part of the thirty-member, FARC negotiating team that had responded to the invitation of Colombian President Juan Manuel Santos, and now he wanted my dad to arrive with a peace proposal.

"Friends: I think this is the opportune moment for you to come to an agreement and arrive at the table with a peace proposal for the Colombians, headed up by Martin [my dad]. This will open the door for us to continue to develop the Friend's Plan. Greetings. May God continue to enlighten your thoughts, Noel."

My dad had been invited to the island.

# CHAPTER 13

# General Barrero

Luis Humberto Montejo, a close friend of my father's and the former Governor of Boyacá – one of the most beautiful and prosperous departments in Colombia – arrived at our apartment in Bogotá precisely when my parents were discussing what they should do regarding the most recent invitation to the island. Striking while the iron is hot is something my father learned from my grandfather and has always put in practice. If it had been up to my dad, he would have taken the very next flight to the island (that very night most likely) without thinking twice about the consequences. I believe it was providential that Luis Humberto arrived at that precise moment. Being a diplomat in every sense of the word, he knew the consequences of talking to terrorists without the proper approval of the government. He told my dad that he needed to be wise about how to proceed.

"People have been thrown in jail for less," Luis Humberto stated. "We need to make the government and the army feel that they are part of this."

My dad thought about it for a while and asked, "What do you suppose I should do?"

They discussed all the possibilities and the different trustworthy people who had direct access to the president when Luis Humberto said, "I would contact General Barrero and tell him everything. Then he can talk to President Santos himself and keep him properly informed. That way the government and the army won't feel excluded from what is going on."

My mom exclaimed, "Finally, a good idea!"

The next day, my dad and Luis Humberto were on a plane for the military brigade in Cali to meet with General Leonardo Barrero, commander of the western task force of the Colombian Armed Forces.

# CHAPTER 14

# Fransisco Vergara's Kidnapping

My dad's friendship with General Leonardo Barrero had begun almost a decade before in February 2005. It was strengthened when a good friend of my dad's, named Fransisco Vergara, was kidnapped by the FARC. It was during several good-willed attempts at a peace initiative that Fransisco Vergara, a renowned Colombian lawyer, was taken captive. What was supposed to have been an amiable talk between Fransisco and my dad and some of the middle-ranking commanders in the FARC movement turned into a hostage situation.

They took both of them deep into the jungle, and at the end of the trail, the guerrillas turned to my dad and said, "You are free to go, but this man stays with us." My dad begged them to take him instead, but it was no use. I saw my dad age ten years during the six long months of Fransisco's captivity. It seemed as if he neither slept nor ate until finally he was able to get him released. During that time, I followed my dad up and down the mountains and into the jungles, filming everything with my Canon XL1 camera. If ever anyone was to have a friend, a worthwhile friend, I cannot think of a better one than my dad. He stopped at nothing to get his friend out of the terrible situation and managed to get participation from all sides of the Friendship Plan to help get him out.

Some days seemed unreal because my dad and I would eat

breakfast with Noel and his guerrilla fellow commanders, go down the mountain and have lunch with the head paramilitary leaders to see how they could help, and then in the evening meet up for dinner with the general of the area. General Barrero proved to be an unconditional friend. He allowed us to put a radio station on one of his high mountain military sites that broadcasted right into the area where it was thought Fransisco was being held.

The FARC front that was holding him captive got hit on all sides. On the one hand, our radio station with intense messages was beaming right into their camp. On the other hand, the army surrounded them and forced them into a checkmate. And on another more discreet side, Noel was sending them letters and talking to his superiors, saying they had kidnapped a person who was his friend and whose only wrong had been to try to initiate peace talks of some sort; saying they needed to let him go.

Fransisco was doing his part by being a very obstinate, outspoken, upper class lawyer, and after a few months of having him call his captors on all their flaws, I think they were happy to get rid of him. Despite the extreme difficulties, the sovereign hand of God was above everything anyone could ever devise against us, and Fransisco Vergara was released from captivity.

## CHAPTER 15

# God and the Colombians Will Know How to Thank You...

The Marxist guerrilla movement is founded on atheism. Decades back, when the FARC started, my dad prayed every night for six months that God would send them the gospel. He thought maybe that meant getting a tract or a Bible in their hands, but he never imagined God would send an actual person, much less that he would be that person. When he found himself tied to a tree, having been kidnapped by them, he asked God why He would allow such a terrible thing to happen, and the Lord responded, "Weren't you the one who asked me to send them the gospel? *You* are the missionary."

He has since had several fleeting encounters with top commanders and many chances to talk to the smaller and even medium level leaders, but he was praying God would open the door for him to have an in with the head honchos of the movement, because he knew if they could change, the whole movement would. And over the past fourteen years, my dad has aimed content of entire radio stations at the top guerrilla leaders.

Now many of the main leaders were all on one island – Cuba. It was a golden opportunity. My dad needed to be wise and use this to show them firsthand the power of God, so there could be no question of whether or not He existed and whether or not He loves them. God showed my dad that the man for the job was Albert Luepnitz. Albert's response to my dad's surprise phone call was, "Russell, you're crazy! But if that is what God wants, then I will go."

A prophet told Albert he was going to see his guardian angel on the trip. On January 3, 2013, my dad, Albert, and Doctor Fernando Torres headed off to Cuba. Doctor Fernando is the real life character in the film we made and one of my family's closest friends. He is the first person my dad calls when somebody, caught in the crossfire of the war, is dying. Whether it is a friend or foe, he does what he can for them, walking for days through the most terrible war zones just to save their lives, without receiving a penny. These wounded men and women would have otherwise died. I know this is something that does not go unnoticed by some of the guerrilla commanders, and this was part of the reason my dad was being invited.

Every person in my family has a story of one time or other when we were literally dying and Doctor Fernando knew exactly what to do to get us better.

January 3rd was the exact same date that my dad had gotten released from his kidnapping twenty-nine years before, and it also fell upon another very special anniversary. Forty-nine years before, in 1964, my dad (an eight-year-old) and his family arrived in Colombia for the very first time as missionaries. The FARC movement was founded that same year only a few months later. This was obviously very significant to him.

On the plane, they upgraded Albert to first class and there his guardian angel appeared to him. This was going to prove to be an important trip. Noel and Yuri met them at the airport and took them to their hotel. Yuri is one of the top guerrilla commanders of the eastern bloc of the FARC who had been listening to our radio station for six years. Every day Noel and Yuri would show up and ask my dad a bunch of questions and write them in their computer. Apparently, they were taking a report to their top leaders. On the fourth day, as my dad was walking with Noel down the beach and remembering old times, Noel told him they needed to find a way out of this. When they got back to the hotel, it was full of the Cuban police providing security for the three top guerrilla negotiators who were waiting for my dad.

Ivan Marquéz, the main leader, began to talk. He was the same one who had appeared on television a few months before in Oslo. Through years of experience, my dad knows enough not to interrupt them while they are giving their communist speech. Ivan came right to the point where they go on about materialism and atheism when he stopped his talk and said, "But Martin, we're different now. We believe in God." This surprised my dad and opened the opportunity for him to tell them about Albert. They said they wanted to meet him. Over the remaining days, Albert, my dad, Doctor Fernando and the top guerrillas became very good friends, and they witnessed many extraordinary miracles firsthand. Ivan summed it all up when he told my dad, Albert, and Doctor Fernando with tears in his eyes, "Now I know that God loves me. Jesus is Lord."

Noel's summary of the trip can be found in a message he wrote to my dad right after the events:

My great friend, you could almost say we are celebrating here. There have been many important advances and good optimism on both sides. Surely, God and our friends are helping us. We learned a lot from their visit. They left us a good path to follow and a transcendental teaching. My friend, I hope you never separate yourself from God or from having patience and talent. They are some of the great merits you have been able to achieve through the experiences you have lived. God and the Colombians will know how to thank you.

# CHAPTER 16

# The Private Meeting

I didn't witness all of the miracles, but we were eager to hear the stories when Albert, my dad, and Doctor Fernando got back. What I did begin to notice was that for the very first time in history, Ivan Márquez and the other negotiators, including the top commander named Timochenko who was in Venezuela, began to talk about facing and recognizing their victims. I read an article in Semana – one of the main magazines – written by a Colombian journalist named Maria Jimena Duzán that confirmed this. She had adopted a pessimistic view of the whole situation when she interviewed Ivan in Oslo back in October.

But when she interviewed him again six months later in Havana, she wrote, "The Ivan Márquez that I found in Havana did not speak to me like the warrior we had seen in Norway." She reported she came back to a completely different Ivan, an Ivan who was willing to face the victims, whereas before when she had talked to him, he didn't even recognize they had any.

Ivan told the reporter on this occasion, "Everyone thinks we are like stones, that we can't change – that we don't listen – and that is not true." I smiled as I read the article. Even the reporters who have the reputation of being very skeptical were getting a whiff of what God was beginning to do, but they were completely clueless as to what had happened.

I have very little hope that this peace process will ever go through. Even if it does, as long as there are people's selfish interests involved on each side, I doubt it would actually benefit the country. A war does not cure itself like that. No, a change must come first, from within each and every heart. That is the sole reason my family and I have been willing to sacrifice our lives on so many trips to dangerous war zones throughout the country.

And this was why we were in Cuba. The change the Lord Jesus is capable of doing in every heart does not exclude anyone who is willing to surrender their hearts to the Creator of the universe. Peace is not something you can sign on paper. To have peace in the midst of a war – in spite of a war – is to have real peace. I am a witness to how God has given me and my family faith and peace and hope, even in the most unbearable and impossible circumstances.

One normal afternoon, after a day full of work in our small, at-home recording studio, my dad called my mom and me up to his room for a private meeting. He closed the door behind him, locked it, and said with a grin on his face, "Albert and Doctor Fernando and I have been invited back to the island. I was thinking it might be a good idea to take the two of you."

## CHAPTER 17

# The Island

It is hard to explain what it's like to go to a place like Cuba for the first time. It is a little intimidating. After all, the only thing I had ever heard of it is that it has a strict government; the citizens are restricted in things like food and religion; and you get stuck in jail for killing a cow. Although I don't doubt those things and many more are true, I was able to see a side of the island I hadn't known before. For one, the people there are the most beautiful, friendly, kind people you will ever meet. All it takes is one piece of candy to make a friend. You feel as though you've been transported back fifty years in time when music was just better and cars looked a lot nicer.

There are expert musicians in every restaurant or on the beach that make your day. The beaches are some of the prettiest I have ever seen. And, there is no Internet. There are no people mindlessly staring into their phones all day, who aren't interacting with the actual people around them. No need for anyone else, but the person who is right in front of you. It is clean and we found we could walk with complete safety at any time.

I am used to people from outside only seeing the worst in Colombia, because all they see is what is on the news. They think Pablo Escobar, drugs, death, and mafia when they think of my country. And although no one can deny that is all true, there is so much more not many people know. Hilario Deluchi, a Colombian-Argentinian music composer, described it perfectly when he said, "How do I explain to people who don't know my country, that in Colombia, joy is stronger than war?"

This was similar to the side of Cuba I was discovering. I admit that the airport was a little intimidating when I went through customs, but as soon as I got out and went to the bathroom, I made friends with all the maids in there. Where else would people be so friendly in an airport bathroom? The first thing they asked me was if I was from Colombia. I said "Yes." They love Colombians and Americans, and I was a little of both. That made their day, and meeting friendly Cuban ladies made mine too.

We arrived around midnight, and Noel and Yuri were waiting for us. It was a long drive to the house we would stay in. When we got there, it looked like an old run-down building. We went to bed that night without really seeing what kind of a place we were in. I got up from my bed the next morning only to wake up to the most spectacular view of the ocean. The house had an old cement deck overlooking the sea. It was as if we were on a boat. No shore, just water from the point where the house and the deck ended. They served us an abundant breakfast of the sweetest mangos, pineapples, and bananas I had ever tasted. Soon the cook realized I loved mangoes and had a cut-up mango waiting for me every time I walked into the kitchen. She was a sweet old lady.

There were patches of blue, crystal clear water. Watching the sun set on one side of the ocean and the city of Havana on the other side every afternoon was magical. For three days, we toured the country with Noel and our Cuban friend, Ernesto. It was fun taking pictures with Albert, my dad, mom, and Noel in the most classic cars from the '40s and '50s. It seemed a bit surreal, not just because of the place we were in, but because of the people we were with. I was touring the island with two of the main characters of *La Montaña*. I felt as if at any moment a film director would come out of hiding and say, "Cut!" and make us do the whole scene over again.

As the days went by, we began having deeper and deeper talks with Noel and Yuri. Noel said he had watched the movie we made about him and my dad and absolutely loved it. He was like a little kid telling us of all the rest of the adventures the two of them had had. His leader, Ivan, asked him if everything in the film was true and Noel responded, "Not only is it true, but it's only a small part of everything that happened!" The openness and respect I found in Noel and Yuri (these tough guerrilla men) toward what my dad and Albert had to say amazed me. Watching my dad and Noel reminisce and laugh for hours telling us of all the things God had done with them in the past was awesome. They told stories I had never heard before. Then Noel would turn to me, smile, and say, "How else could you explain why this all works out for us? Someone is obviously helping us."

"Someone" was his way of saying God. Noel and others have watched how my dad and the people working with him had a perfect safety record for thirty years, in the midst of the most intense war zone you can imagine. Noel knew that only God could have done this. Noel has a mentality of trying to see how many people he can save instead of how many he can destroy, even if he has to go against the thinking of some of his comrades. This is a mark of the work of God in his heart. After witnessing countless miracles, he could also affirm beyond the shadow of a doubt that God loves him. Yuri is of the same mind as are countless guerrillas, paramilitaries, and soldiers listening to our radio broadcasts over the length and breadth of Colombia.

I began to notice in Noel's talk that every time he said "them" or "they," he meant his other companions in the FARC, but when he said "us" or "we," it was always referring to him, my dad, and others touched by God. I thought, "Wow, although if asked, he will always say he is a communist, it is obvious that subconsciously he sympathizes and is more a part of what God is doing than he knows."

Noel became our ally on the island. After only a few months of having received the movie, he had already made over 600 copies of it, and in only a matter of days, the whole neighborhood we had been staying in had seen it and loved it. In Cuba, 600 copies might as well be 60,000 copies because everyone shares. He also made sure all the leaders of the FARC delegation watched it too. He wrote us one time and said, "The commanders are watching the movie. They haven't said a word, and neither have I."

Albert always says he does not take sides in war, and he is faithful to his word. He will pray for a guerrilla, a soldier, or a paramilitary, and the Lord is the one who decides whether or not they get healed. But disappointed, he told me on the island, "Alethia, I don't understand what is happening here. The Colombian government has seen me praying for tens of thousands of their soldiers for almost thirty years now, and they have seen how most of them have been healed. They know who I am; yet they aren't the ones calling me, inviting me to please come and participate. These communist guerrillas are. Right now, I am disgusted with the government. These guys make them look bad."

# CHAPTER 18

# The Grace to Love Them

The day came for us to meet some of the head honchos of the FARC guerrilla movement. A bus came to our house and picked us all up at around four o'clock in the evening. We drove for what seemed a long time through the most humble neighborhoods I've seen in Havana along the edge of the ocean. My mom turned to Yuri and Noel and jokingly said, "You guys better not be kidnapping us!" They laughed at the joke, although it did hint at a terrible reality.

My mom is extremely forward with these guys, and at times I felt like crawling under a blanket and hiding because of her blatant directness toward them. But she spoke for all of us. At one point she said to Yuri, "The reason so many Colombians, like me, fear this peace treaty is we don't want to become another country like Cuba or Venezuela. If you guys can prove that this is not going to happen, then I bet any one of us would support what is going on here, but you haven't."

On another occasion she said, "I voted for Uribe twice, and I never regretted it." She was referring to Álvaro Uribe Vélez, the former president of Colombia who had been elected two times from 2002 to 2010. It was bold of her to say this, since he was the one who had caused them the most harm in recent years. She continued, "I didn't vote for him because he promised me a house, or good health care, or so many of the things that cause people to vote. The only thing that stuck with me out of his speech was that he was going to do away with you all. Please don't take this personally. I do not have anything personal against anyone of you, but you have to realize that the FARC movement has made mistakes that have caused much of the Colombian population to think the same way I do. For one, what a terrible mistake you make in kidnapping people."

At this, Noel and Yuri said the FARC hadn't kidnapped anyone, but the hostages they had were merely "political prisoners."

My mom responded, "I don't care what you want to call it. I call it kidnapping, and I had to live through one. I wouldn't want anyone to have to go through what I went through. You've destroyed entire families." At this, they were completely silent. She continued, "The only reason why I'm here is because God has given my husband a profound love for you people. Something I do not understand. But since I am his wife, I stand by him no matter how crazy it seems to me."

We arrived at what seemed like a humble Cuban cement house along the ocean. A friendly lady ushered us in, and we went up a flight of stairs and were surprised to see a nicely laid out banquet in a beautiful room with a balcony that over-looked the ocean. They served us typical Cuban cuisine. Doctor Fernando and his wife, along with Albert, my parents, Steve (an American reporter), Noel, Yuri, and I were all waiting for the FARC leaders to arrive as we casually talked about mundane things. We watched the sun set over the ocean, and as soon as it got dark, we saw a big, bullet-proof van pull up in front of the house, and three very recognized and hated characters, whom I had only seen in the news, got out. I suddenly became very nervous. Now that I look back, I think that God in that moment was giving me the grace to do what I couldn't do on my own. He was giving me the grace to love them.

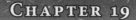

## CHAPTER 19

# Meeting Ivan

We heard the trio walk up the stairs. Ivan Márquez was the number two commander of the FARC movement. Jesús Santrich was another main leader, who always wears dark sunglasses to cover up his blindness. The other was a woman named Maritza, a widow to the former commander of the FARC and now Ivan's companion. I was expecting an awkward moment when they came into the room, but to my surprise it was like the reunion of old, long-time friends. Ivan, Santrich, and Maritza walked in with huge smiles on their faces and gave my dad, Albert, and the doctor the biggest, most affectionate hugs. This, coming from the tough, hardened guys I had seen in the news, took me a little off guard.

There is much you can tell about a person by just shaking hands and saying hi. When I shook hands with Ivan, I felt he was barely coming out of a dark past that still had a grip on him, but he was headed in the right direction. My dad took the opportunity to introduce me to Ivan. "This is my daughter Alethia; she and her sister directed *La Montaña.*"

I thought, "Great way to throw me into the water, Dad."

But Ivan looked at me and said, "I watched the movie. I loved seeing those mules. The cinematography amazed me. Congratulations." I was beginning to learn that contrary to what I had seen on TV, Ivan was an innate diplomat. I said thank you and we all sat down around the long table to talk.

Albert began to talk to them about the peace process. He told them the only way it would work is if they did it God's way and not man's way. God's way has to do with forgiveness. The only way we can truly forgive is to surrender to the Lord Jesus Christ. It is as we repent and trust Him that we realize we have been forgiven. He is the only one who can help us forget the hurts and injuries of the past. Then we will not hold on to things or take vengeance into our own hands, because He will enable us to overcome evil with good.

Steve, the reporter, asked them political questions about the drug trade and the peace negotiations. As they talked to Steve, Ivan began to send each one of his men in to be prayed for by Albert in a private room. I watched as Albert prayed and my dad translated. One of his bodyguards was healed of a hernia in his stomach. Then Maritza walked in the room and Albert prayed for her. She wanted him to pray for her heart, in an emotional sense.

At the table while talking to Albert and my mom, Maritza told them that she didn't want any demons to be influencing them in the peace talks. Albert told her that all she had to do was pray about it and put herself in Jesus' hands. She shyly turned to my mom with a napkin and a pen in her hand and said, "Can you ask Albert to write down a prayer for me to pray every day before we start the peace talks. See, I don't know how to pray."

This melted my mom's heart and she said, "All you have to do is be honest with God and tell Him you want Him to take over and He will. It doesn't matter how you pray, as long as your heart is honest." Then Albert began to tell her a simple prayer, and she fervently wrote it down on her little napkin.

The next person who went into the little private room for prayer was Santrich, the blind leader. Albert asked him if he had continued to pray for his own eyes. Santrich took his sunglasses off and like a child put both hands over his eyes and said, "Every night, I pray that my eyes would be healed in the name of Jesus." I was seeing a side of these people almost no one had ever seen – the spiritual side. A day before, I had sent him an audio Bible and some Narnia radio novels we produced in the recording studio with Yuri. I asked him if he had received them, and he immediately changed his tone and said in a commanding voice, "No, I didn't receive them. Who did you send them with?"

I thought, "Shoot, now I got Yuri in trouble and who knows what will happen to him." While trying to choose my words carefully, I said, "I sent them with Yuri, but it was just about a day ago."

Immediately he changed his manner again back to a smile and said, "Oh, that explains it. See, we've been busy these past few days. But I'm looking forward to listening to them. I like painting and I've made two paintings, one of a saxophone and the other of a piano. I'd like to give you one of them."

Painting and music were not what I had imagined myself talking about with these guys. I said, "Thank you so much. I used to play the saxophone and the piano. They were my favorite instruments."

He said, "The saxophone is also my favorite instrument and I love playing it." I gave him the soundtrack of our movie and explained to him how every character had an instrument that portrayed each one of them. He smiled and said, "Thank you. I will send you the painting sometime before you leave."

I led him back to where Ivan, Steve, my dad, and all the rest were talking. The next person who came into the private room for prayer was Ivan. As my dad translated, Albert prayed for a blood clot he had in his leg. After the prayer, he couldn't feel the pain in his leg anymore. Then he asked us to pray God would give him wisdom. My dad and I both prayed for him. I prayed Colombia would see a new day of justice and righteousness. Everyone talks about justice and righteousness but seldom knows that the only one who impersonates those things and can give it is the Lord Jesus. My dad and Albert began to talk to him. All I could think of was the theme of *La Montaña* that had been about how the least likely ones who had done the most harm (the bad guys) were going to be given a chance to do right again, and God was going to use them. As I looked at Ivan, I thought, "He is definitely one of the least likely. Who would've thought God would be so literal."

Ivan interrupted my thoughts and looked at me as if to make sure I was paying attention to the conversation. He asked, "Alethia, do you think we are the bad ones and the government is good?"

I remembered something a very dear friend of mine named Anibal Hernandez had told me once while discussing the peace negotiations. He said, "Alethia, there is no good side in these negotiations. There are just two sides of things: the government on the one hand does bad things legally and under the premise of the law, and the guerrillas do bad things outside of the law, but both are as bad as the other. The only ones who have the possibility of doing something good are those who let God reign in their hearts. That is the only way justice and righteousness can flow as a mighty river."

It was the perfect response to this question, so I said, "Both are bad. The only ones who have the possibility of doing something good are those who get closer to God, because He is the only one who can do anything good, and He can work through us if we let Him. Right now, the ball in your court because God is giving you a chance. He hasn't given the ones on the side of the government the same opportunity. What will you do?"

He looked from side to side, and I could tell he felt a little uncomfortable. Then he said, "We have another meeting. I guess it's time to go."

Later, I sent him a letter and one of the things I said to him was that like King Solomon, he had asked God for wisdom, but King David had asked God to give him a clean heart. I wrote, "If you compare the reign of David with the reign of Solomon, King David's kingdom surpassed King Solomon's because having a clean heart is better than having wisdom."

A few days passed and I received a most beautiful painting from Santrich – a saxophone with the most brilliant, vivid colors with a sun shining on it. I can't paint that well and I can see! On the back of the painting, he wrote, "For Alethia, with profound hopes for peace. Fraternally, Santrich."

What I am about to say is a complete paradox to the image everyone has of him. In the news, he comes off as a mean, obnoxious man with no compassion for the war's victims. But if I had met him out of context, without knowing who he was, I would have thought he was a dear, sweet person with a very tender heart toward God and all of us. Yes, I will probably be hated for saying that, but it is what I saw, and I can find no other explanation than the fact that God is beginning to work in his life.

# CHAPTER 20

# The "Fetus"

We were staying in a little neighborhood called Jaimanitas which was right across from the huge piece of land where they said Fidel Castro lived. A Cuban named Ernesto was our next-door neighbor and designated driver, recommended to us by Noel. My dad has an eye for finding the good in people no matter who they are or what flaws they may have, and one of the things he has always said regarding Noel is he has the capability of finding really valuable people, whether it was in the mountains of Colombia, or in this case, on the island.

For years Ernesto had been one of Fidel and Raul's top secret police, and now he was taking us everywhere in his little white '60s vehicle. Ernesto was the epitome of a Cuban man – humble, honest, protective, good-natured, and ever displaying a deep yearning to discover new horizons. We were his window into another world. "Americans? Cubans don't hate Americans. The government may hate them, but secretly Americans are our favorite people. Americans *and* Colombians of course," he said while looking at my mom. "Our least favorite people are the Muslims. What's up with their clothes? It's weird."

Never afraid to speak his mind with us, he made sure we saw the best of the island. One day he said, "Alethia, if you can bring me anything from Colombia, bring me garbanzo beans."

"You mean you don't have such a common thing as garbanzo beans here?"

"We do, but it is a delicacy. Most people like me can't afford it."

On our first time out in his car, he said, "Hold on, I need gas." I was expecting he would stop in a gas station, but he pulled up in front of an old, run-down house. An older man came out with a gallon of gas and poured it into his car with a small hose. Ernesto said, "I would go to the gas station, but it's too expensive. Most things here in Cuba work illegally, because we can't afford anything legal." After days of him driving us everywhere and telling us about the island, I asked him about his wife. He said casually, "My wife? She's in the hospital."

"The hospital!" I said. "What's wrong?"

"Oh, nothing, it's just that the fetus is trying to come out before time because her womb is opening up. So she has to stay lying down in the hospital with her legs up on a board so it doesn't come out three-months premature." I thought about the word he used. For him, the unborn baby was merely a fetus.

I had an idea. "Ernesto, I want to visit her with Albert and my mom."

He shrugged his shoulders and said, "Sure. Just get in the car and we'll go."

I got Albert and my mom, and as Ernesto drove us there, he spoke of the hospital to which we were headed with great pride. "The architect designed it in a way that if you look at it from the air, it has the shape of a vagina because its specialty is in maternity."

We arrived at what seemed to be an abandoned building. It was obvious that nothing on the island had been repainted since the 1950s, and the same was the case with this hospital. We walked in, and there was no one in the reception area, no guards, no nurses, and no secretaries. All we saw were long, silent halls with old green and white paint. Once in a while we noticed a Fidel Castro poster with a quote that said something like, "Your healthcare is free but it costs us such and such to…" And it would list the amount it would cost the government for specific surgeries.

As we strolled down the long forbidding halls, I saw what I thought was a street bum lying across two cement hospital chairs. As soon as he heard us walk by, he got up from his nap and said, "Sorry, visiting hours are over." Ernesto covertly handed him a few coins, and we continued on our way through the desolate halls to the most macabre looking elevator I had ever seen. I was not thrilled, as my experience of getting stuck in elevators flashed through my mind.

On one occasion, I got stuck in an elevator with twelve of my girlfriends. We thought it was a fun idea to see how many of us could cram into a six-person elevator. After two girls literally fainted because of lack of air, we were forced to take turns cramming our noses down a small crack that allowed us a little bit of oxygen. After two hours, somebody finally rescued us, and we had to drag the girls who were unconscious out before the doors closed again.

What made matters worse on this occasion was that the light bulb in the elevator was out, and as soon as the doors shut, we found ourselves in utter darkness. There were empty holes in the spaces that once held the buttons where you could choose the destination floor. After about thirty seconds of my dark past with elevators trying to come back and haunt me, we arrived at the third floor. As we walked the long corridors, I looked into each room and never saw a nurse, a doctor, or anyone who resembled a person who knew what they were doing. There were rooms that were so ominous and desolate they looked like the perfect set for one of Alfred Hitchcock's movies.

So this was the great health care system everyone raved about, and many countries tried to imitate. Finally, we arrived at a small room painted years before with a light green color, which contained two old wooden beds. It seemed like a room you could find in the humble house of a poor neighborhood. There were no oxygen tanks, blood pressure monitors, or anything that remotely looked like it could be normal hospital equipment. It was just a room with two small beds.

Ernesto's wife lay on the bed nearest the grey window. She was beautiful. It is one thing to be pretty when you are in your best state with nice clothes on and at least a little blush. But to be sick and pregnant in a dreary hospital and still look nice, now that is something else. She gave us a warm smile and invited us in. Ernesto introduced her to us, and I asked her if she would like Albert to pray for her. She nodded her head in approval. Albert sat next to where she was lying and said, "Just place your hand on the area of the problem, and I will place my hands over yours, and we will pray." Although I have no way of knowing what she was feeling as he prayed over her, I knew something profound was taking place because she began to cry. Albert turned to me and with a smile said, "I feel a strong anointing coming from my hands. It feels like low voltages of electricity."

When he was finished praying, a black lady who was lying in the bed next to her said, "What are you doing?"

My mom replied, "He was praying for her."

The lady exclaimed, "I need prayer too! Please, can he pray for me?"

Albert laid his hands on her, and as soon as he was done praying, we rushed down the hospital halls toward the exit. Poor Albert had just read an article about a Canadian being thrown into jail by Cuban authorities for having prayed for someone. It was no wonder he wanted to get out of there before anyone else asked him for prayer.

# CHAPTER 21

# Freddy

O n our last day on the island, another guerrilla from the negotiating table showed up at our house. No one introduced us, and I just found him there on the deck overlooking the ocean. Had I known who he was, perhaps I would not have asked him so many questions.

"What part of Cuba are you from?"

"I'm not from Cuba."

"Really? So where are you from?"

"I'm from Colombia."

"Oh great! What part?"

I still had no clue whatsoever who he was, although I guess I should have figured it out.

"I'm from San Martin."

"San Martin! That's where my mom is from! And my grandma and most of my uncle's family live in that town! Do you know that my Uncle Raúl and Aunt Mabel make the most delicious homemade ice cream ever? Have you tried it? It's famous."

"No, I haven't been there for thirty years."

I thought that was weird.

"So, where have you been this whole time?"

"Cali."

"Cali, I love that city; Valle del Cauca is one of the most beautiful areas in the country. What do you do in Cali?"

"I run operations."

"What kind of operations?"

"Oh, just operations."

He "ran operations." I was beginning to catch on.

"What are you doing here?"

"It's my liver; my commanders told me to come here for Albert to pray for me. I have hospital appointments every day, and the doctors don't know what's wrong."

I looked at him and noticed that he was extremely pale and yellow-looking.

"How long have you been in Cuba?"

"Just a few days."

"Were you one of the ones who recently arrived with Pablo Catatumbo?"

He nodded his head in affirmation.

"Will you give him something from me?"

He said yes, and I handed him a copy of *La Montaña* and wrote, "Para Pablo Catatumbo."

Pablo Catatumbo is another one of their top commanders who is part of the FARC's secretariat. They had brought him in for the peace negotiations. I was talking to one of his right-hand men known as "Freddy" who had been in charge of their whole military operations in Cauca, one of the most war-torn areas in the country. Freddy began to give me his communist speech about materialism and justice and how they fought for equality and that there was no God. There was just a material world.

My mom joined the conversation, and we began to tell him about our friend Dudley's discovery. In the '80s, Dudley had been a marine intelligence officer for the US Navy. On one of his missions underneath the great ocean, they intercepted a nearby Russian submarine. The Russians had discovered Noah's Ark. Dudley and the other officers overheard the entire conversation. The Ark was found in Turkey and had made such an impact on the Russians that in order to hide this evidence, they began to remove all the remains of the Ark. To this day, both the United States and Russian governments have kept this information classified and will stop at nothing to keep it hidden.

Dudley did not believe in God back when that happened, nor did this event cause his lack of faith to change, but it was something he never forgot. Years later, when God began to touch him, he was reminded of this incident and began to speak out openly of this discovery. As a result, he has been under constant persecution from none other than the US government. I asked Freddy, the guerrilla commander, "Why do you think people in high government ranks have worked so hard to keep these things a secret?"

I went on to tell him of how archeologists had found the actual wheels of Pharaoh's chariots underneath the Red Sea from when the Egyptians had followed the Israelites and God had parted the waters. Freddy said, "I respect your faith, but I still believe in what I believe."

"I understand that. I would be the same way. It is one thing to be told about something or someone, and it is a whole different story to know things for yourself. The same thing happened with me in regards to you guys. I had always heard about it in the news; the FARC this, the FARC did that, etc. And for years, I heard my dad talk about his interactions with all of you. But deep down inside, I had a dream to see for myself who you really were and what this war was all about. That is why I jumped in my dad's car on the very first trip to visit Noel. I was expecting to find a terrorist, but instead, I found a friend.

"The same thing happens with God. It is not enough to hear me tell you very wonderful stories about Him. It is not enough to hear Evangelicals or Catholics talk to you about Him, because there comes a point in your life when you will want to know who He really is for yourself. You will have to jump into the car, like I did, and find out. The reason we are here on this island is not because of you; it is because of Him. Why would someone like my dad, who was tied to a tree for five months like an animal by your people, come and see you guys? Do you see any of the other people you've kidnapped here, trying to help you out? The only explanation I see for it is that God has given him the capacity to love his enemies."

I told Freddy numerous stories of all the terrible things we had had to live through as a result of their organization. One time, one of their commanders had gotten mad about a book my dad had been distributing and had ordered to have him killed. I said, "We were his hostages for days until God intervened, and the situation got resolved. But God gave me the peace that passes all understanding, and even when they took my dad away from me before my very eyes, I was not afraid."

Freddy's eyes began to water, and he said in a low, almost inaudible voice, more to himself than to me, "This is the most beautiful thing I have ever heard. We have done you so much harm, yet you are here on this island, and you are our friends. Please forgive us for everything."

# CHAPTER 22

# My Favorite Uncle

We returned to Colombia just in time to see my Uncle Raúl Espitia. The best ice cream maker from San Martin, my favorite uncle ever, and my mom's brother had been diagnosed with the worst possible cancer only three weeks before. I remember weeping one night in desperation asking God to please do something. It all seemed so hopeless. But as I look back, I realize God has never left one tear forgotten. He answered my prayer and gave my family hope. I went to visit him before going to the island and brought a beautiful note my sister had written to him about how he would soon see the daughter he had lost and our grandfather.

When I went into his room with my aunt Rosario, he began to have the most terrible attacks on all his bones. My aunt said we needed to pray for him. We did. And my heart pressed me to read Psalm 80 to him. I grabbed the Bible and began to read. Every time I read the verse that says "Turn us again, O God of the hosts, and cause thy face to shine; and we shall be saved," he would shout, "Amen!" and I would continue to read.

The presence of God began to fill the room, and I continued on with Psalm 126. As soon as I finished reading, he fell into a deep, peaceful sleep. Three hours later, he woke up. The first thing he did was give me a huge hug and say, "Thank you so much for praying for me sweetie; I hadn't slept that well in weeks." From that point on, I never shed another tear for him because I knew that since God's hand was in the ordeal, everything would be okay. Every day he would ask my aunt, "When is Albert coming?" It was as if he had to wait until Albert arrived, so he could die in peace.

That Saturday night, we had a family meeting with my extended relatives on my mom's side of the family. My aunt brought my uncle out of his room in a wheelchair. He was deathly pale and just skin and bones. Albert laid hands on him and the whole family began to see a light from within begin to shine through. The deep heaviness of death itself lifted, and I could see that it took all the strength left in him to say, "I forgive anyone who has ever hurt me, and I ask for forgiveness from anyone I have hurt. I love Jesus, and I want him to reign in my heart." He died a few hours later at two o'clock in the morning.

As my grandma was weeping over his grave, my uncle Leonardo said to her, "Cry, mother, cry because it is good to cry, but know our spirit should not remain sad because when Raúl said that last prayer, I saw peace fill his face completely, and I know for certain that he is with God."

God is so faithful! Even in death, He makes it all beautiful.

My uncle died on May 5, 2013, the same day another very close friend – Del Berge, a faithful friend and supporter of this work in Colombia – died of the same type of cancer up in Canada. May they rest in peace.

# CHAPTER 23

## Noel Meets Lisa and Sammy

A few days later, my dad had the idea to send me back to Cuba with my sister Lisa and her husband Samuel Hernandez. Sammy is an economist and my dad's right hand in everything he does. He also turned out to be an excellent actor. When he interpreted my dad's character in the movie, not even my grandma could tell the difference between Sammy and her actual son. We would travel with Steve Salisbury, the American reporter who was writing an article about the peace process.

At first, Lisa was completely against the thought of going. But my mom spoke with her, and as she told my sister of everything she had seen on the island, my mom began to weep, "Listen, I left for Cuba at a time when my brother was dying, and those were my last days with him. Like you, I didn't want to go because frankly I don't have a heart for those people and I would rather be with my brother, but your dad insisted I needed to go and I needed to trust the Lord would take care of Raúl. And He not only took care of him, He showed me what He is doing with those men over there who I wouldn't give a cent for. It was worth it. God is doing something beautiful, and you need to see it."

To make a long story short, we arrived at the same house we had stayed in previously, and when Noel saw Lisa for the first time, it was as if he had seen a long-lost daughter who had come to life again. He hugged her, picked her up, and hugged her again. There were tears in both of their eyes, and Noel began to tell us stories of him and my dad. Then he turned to Sammy, my brother-in-law, and said, "Russell and I have talked about who would take over in our Plan Amigos, when we are too old, and he always told me that you would take over for him. It is a privilege, after all these years, to finally get to meet you." Sammy gave him a fervent heart-felt hug, and they became immediate good friends.

During our time in Cuba, we went out to the beaches and toured the city during the day, and then at night after a long day's work at the negotiating table, Noel and Yuri would come by our house, and we would talk for hours until two or three o'clock in the morning. It was as if they felt at home and comfortable with us. On one night, Steve the reporter asked Noel about his family. Noel pointed at the three of us and said, "See them? They are my family."

One day as Lisa, Sammy, and I were walking through a beautiful park, we saw a group of about ten people gathered under the shade of a gorgeous, flowering tree. As I walked by them, I heard one of the ladies talking. She said, "We need to give thanks to the Lord because we are not confined to four walls. We can praise and give Him thanks here, in His beautiful creation, under this beautiful tree. No one can take that away from us." She had a Bible in her hands, and it looked like she was about to give them all a message.

I saw Sammy sitting on a park bench nearby. We smiled at each other as both of us knew we had been listening to the same thing. When I approached him, Sammy whispered in my ear, "It looks like they are Christians. But we can't say anything to them because we'll get them in trouble. Remember who we're running around with." As we walked by them, Sammy casually said, "God bless you." What would have been a normal remark to anyone in Colombia or the United States was beyond normal in Cuba.

The ladies looked at each other in amazement saying to one another, "Did you hear him? He said, 'God bless you!' He's a Christian! We've found a brother! Come and eat this bread with us!"

Unable to stop and greet them, we kept on walking and Sammy said, "Thank you so much, but we have to go."

On our last night on the island, we asked Noel and Yuri to tell us about the relationship they had with the members of the government's negotiation team. They said, "It's simple. They only recognize us during the peace talks. Right after that, they treat us like complete strangers. Once both sides were invited to a piano concert, and when they heard that we were going, they decided not to go."

Then Yuri said, "But General Mora is kinder to us than the others. One time I crossed paths with him as he was jogging, and he said hi to me. That made me think of how nice it would be if one day in Colombia, we could simply say a kind hello to our enemies as we walked down the street."

That night, I gave Noel three copies of *La Montaña* and said, "These are not for you to give out to your comrades. I want you to pick three people from the government delegation and use this movie to make friends with them." He solemnly nodded as if he had just been given a great mission. I added, "I think that the Noel who was able to make friends with some of his worst enemies – like Cuchillo and Jorge Pirata – can surely make friends with the delegates from the government. It shouldn't be too hard for you."

When we got back to Colombia, my dad and mom began to wonder why Noel had had such a tremendous reaction with the coming of my sister. They came to this conclusion: when my dad was kidnapped, he had a little picture in his wallet of nine-month old Lisa, who was the only child back then, and he would show it to all his captors. Noel remembered this because even on the first trip when I had met him, the first thing he asked my dad was, "Is this the same one?"

My dad said, "No, this is my second daughter."

That conversation is in the movie, and I wrote the story with Lisa exactly how I had lived it. But it is interesting to find that for all these years, Noel had in some way felt the pain of someone who had had to be separated from his only daughter.

# CHAPTER 24

# Tom Howes

Tom Howes had been one of the three American contractors who had been kidnapped by the FARC and held for over five years. After many people like my dad and Uncle Chaddy did everything in their power to get them out, it seemed like the most tremendous impossibility. I think most everyone in the country had given up hope they would ever be free again. Even though we didn't know these three Americans or any of the hundreds of kidnapped people personally, I think every Colombian felt the sorrow and the hopelessness of the situation to some degree.

Perhaps it would have been easier for the country to forgive the atrocities committed in this war had it not been for the kidnappings. For years we would sit and watch the news, and once in a blue moon a picture of some deathly skinny person would come up as proof of life, but nothing would happen beyond that.

Years before in the summer of 2008, my grandparents invited me and my cousin Misty to go on a road trip with them from Minnesota to Alaska. In every town in which we stopped, my grandparents would speak at a church and tell them a little bit about the work they were doing with the Kogi Indian Tribe. (To learn more of their mission work with the Indians read *High Adventure in Colombia* by Chad Stendal or *Minnesota Mom in the Land of the Ancient Mother* by Pat Stendal.) Before our first meeting, my grandma told Misty and me she wanted us to speak at the meetings. Being extremely shy when it comes to speaking in public, we both said we were a little nervous and had never done it before, but if grandma really wanted us to speak, then so be it.

Misty asked me, "What is it that we are supposed to say?"

I told her something my dad had always taught me, "Just say whatever God puts in your heart."

She jokingly replied, "How 'bout I just explain the verse of the Bible that I know how to explain and that's it." We both laughed.

On the day of the meeting, I had a message of something God had shown me recently, and I was prepared to speak on that. However, a few minutes before getting up to the platform, I prayed He would give me the right words to say. When I got up to the pulpit, my mind went blank, and whatever message I had thought I was going to say was completely gone. I began with the first thing that came to my mind. I nervously grabbed the mike and said, "In Colombia there are more than 2,000 people kidnapped, including three Americans who have been held hostage for more than five years. We need to stand up and pray that God would free all of them!" The whole church stood up and prayed with me.

Then my cousin Misty got up after me and said, "This mission teeters on the edge of a knife. It could go either way. For the next few weeks, it is imperative that we continue to pray for the freedom of these three Americans." Little did we know, in that same instance, things were being set in motion for their rescue.

Two weeks later, we arrived at Edmonton and checked into a hotel. This was one of the only times on our trip that we stayed in a hotel because we usually stayed with friends. We would never turn on the news at somebody else's house, but because we were in the hotel, my grandpa turned the TV on as soon as we got into our room. The bold headlines came up: The three Americans had been rescued. As we watched, more extraordinary news appeared: Ingrid Betancourt, the French-Colombian, ex-presidential candidate had also been rescued. Then more good news came up: Eleven more people had also been rescued.

I began to weep uncontrollably. In my whole life as a Colombian watching horrid news reports continually, this was the first time I had ever seen such a divine intervention take place in what seemed a hopeless situation. God had intervened miraculously because He had His eyes on our country. My grandpa turned off the TV and we all thanked God profoundly for the new hope. That was the quickest answer to prayer I had ever had, but of course it didn't seem as quick to the families of the people who had been kidnapped. They had been praying and weeping for years.

What happened was the Colombian military had disguised themselves as Marxist guerrilla rebels and had managed to get all the hostages into their helicopter before the guerrillas realized it was a hoax. Thirty seconds after the helicopter took off, the professional soldiers began untying the hostages and said, "We are the Colombian army and you are free!" It was one of the most brilliant rescues in history. This was later known as Operation *Jaque* (Checkmate). The former hostages started crying and jumping and were so happy they almost brought the helicopter down! It was a great day for the whole country. Hope was rekindled. Good things were possible once again. The country was on the right track.

On the same trip my grandma, Misty, and I were eating breakfast in a little café somewhere along the road between Canada and Alaska. We saw a sad-looking lady waiting on the tables. She was dressed in black and had a nose ring, a tongue ring, and every kind of ring you can imagine on her face. But beyond the outer appearance, what struck us was that she looked depressed and lonely. My grandma whispered to us, "Wouldn't it be nice if one day we could be like those soldiers in the helicopter and say to people who are in bondage like this lady, 'We are the army of God, and you are free!'"

Three years later in 2011, Deanne Alford, an American news reporter, called my dad and said, "I interviewed Tom Howes, and he said that during his captivity he would listen to your radio station through one of the Galcom radios. He also said he received some of your books through the parachute drops and would be interested in meeting you." My dad and I were speaking at a Galcom convention in Tampa, only a two-hour drive from where he was. Without hesitation, we drove to his house to meet him. It was a beautiful house next to the ocean. When no one answered the doorbell, we walked through the backyard and found Mr. Tom Howes cleaning his pool. He gave us a warm smile and welcomed us in. From then on it was an immediate friendship.

One of the first things he said was that he had listened to the messages on the radio for years, and his favorite one was "Noah's Ark." Even though I didn't say anything, I was thrilled to hear that. I have also listened to the messages broadcast through the radio station for years, and the one that stuck out to me the most was always "Noah's Ark." I never forgot it, until one day I transcribed it, and my dad put it into his most recent book called *The Seven Trumpets and the Seven Thunders*. Tom said he had received many of the books because they had been dropped onto them through parachutes. One of the memorable ones he had read until it was completely worn out was *The Last of the Giants*, which also happened to be one of my favorite books. As he was putting chlorine in the pool, he asked, "Russell, how long were you held hostage?"

My dad replied, "Only five months. Nothing compared to what you went through."

Tom stopped what he was doing and said, "No, it is something. The first five months are the hardest. That's when they break you. After that, you're already used to it."

My dad remarked, "The hardest part for me to get through was the could've, would've, should've. You always wonder about what could have happened had I done this or that. But then the only way you can rest is that you just have to trust that into God's hands."

I was intrigued. Here were two American legends talking about their experiences deep in the jungles of Colombia, a place not a lot of people from outside knew anything about.

We continued our talk in the most amazing restaurant by the ocean, where I was served crab, my favorite food. My dad and Tom both started discussing different airplane models and after a while, Tom looked at me with a twinkle in his eyes and said, "Alethia, is all this plane talk boring you?"

I smiled. He had read my mind. I replied, "Yes, kind of."

"Yeah, I learned that while I was kidnapped. Before then, I thought everyone was like me, that everyone wanted to hear about all the different airplanes and the engines, until one day Marc woke me up to the cruel reality that people who aren't pilots don't really care." Tom Howes, was kidnapped together with two friends named Marc Gonsalves and Keith Stansell.

We laughed and then we started talking about all the different experiences he had had in the jungle. I asked him if there was any bitterness or resentment in him toward his kidnappers, and his response surprised me. He said, "Life is too short to waste it on resentments. I don't have time to be bitter."

When we arrived at his house, he gave us each a copy of the book he had written. My dad gave him a copy of *Rescue the Captors.* I took a picture as they signed their books for one another.

The book these three Americans wrote, *Out Of Captivity*, is one of the saddest books I have ever read. Some pages just made me cry. One story that captivated me was when Tom Howes told about a sixteen-year-old guerrilla who had heatstroke and could not hike anymore. The three Americans looked at each other in an indecisive moment. Why should they help someone who was causing them so much harm? No one would have condemned them had they not helped her. Everyone would have understood. But they decided to help her. The line that stuck with me was when Tom wrote, "Just because we were being treated inhumanely didn't mean that we had to give up our humanity."

It is one thing to read stories of the Jews, for example, who were exterminated by Hitler, because you know that it already happened. It is history. At least that's what I hope. But to read each page of what these three Americans had to go through and know that it is still happening even now is horrible. People are still being held in the jungle with chains around their necks, not able to see their loved ones, completely separated from life as they had known it.

I remember what a friend, whose dad had been killed by the paramilitaries, had the courage to do. She sent the paramilitary leader who had ordered her dad's death a Christmas present. In a letter she wrote him, "My Christmas gift to you is forgiveness. I forgive you for having killed my father. I hope God gives you the grace to forgive yourself." A reporter asked her what she thought of the hostages, and she said, "My hope is that they would discover true freedom, the kind God gives, because then it won't matter whether they are in captivity or not."

My friend Anibal Hernandez has always said that the Colombian national anthem is a prophecy for our nation, and

I believe him. One of the lines is: "*La humanidad entera que entre cadenas gime, comprende las palabras del que murió en la cruz.*" Translated it means: "All of mankind, which is groaning in chains, understands the words of the one who died on the cross."

Our chains can come in different forms. It might be something as literal as an actual chain, like so many people have had to go through, or something like a job or a sickness. My dad discovered true freedom when he was held in captivity with a chain around his neck. He was given a Bible, and God began to speak to him in a way he had never experienced before. The national anthem was being fulfilled literally in him, because in chains, he began to comprehend the words of one who died on the cross.

These events proved to be the beginning of a great new friendship, and I never hesitate to contact Tom Howes each time I am in Florida.

A week after my trip to Cuba with Lisa and Sammy, I was on a plane for our 2013 USA *La Montaña* tour. I was going on a road trip with Lisa, Sammy, my two brothers, and my closest friends who helped us make the movie. Our mission was to promote the film to all our friends from Florida to Minnesota. Our last stop was to be New York City because I was enrolled to study photography at the New York Film Academy.

My good friend Melissa picked me up in Miami. As she drove me to her house, she said, "Hold on, I need to stop at the supermarket for some milk." It was all I could do to fight back the tears as I walked into the Publix. After where I had just been, it was like going into food heaven. There was every sort of product you could imagine in one normal, small supermarket. I had been in Cuba only a week before, and I could not help but compare it. Only fifty miles south was a country where garbanzo beans were an unaffordable delicacy, and candy or chips were a rare specialty.

One thousand copies of the movie arrived at our hotel. Before beginning our trip north, we decided to stay a few days in Orlando to prepare and visit Disney World.

I remembered that Tom Howes lived nearby. From the phone in my hotel room, I called him up. A warm, friendly voice answered, "Hello, movie mogul! It's nice to hear from you again."

"It's good to hear from you too!"

I told him I was near his house with some friends and would like to stop by and visit in the next few days. He said he would have a barbeque ready for us. Then we started talking about politics and Colombia, and he asked me what I thought about the peace negotiations in Cuba. I said, "Well, that's for the birds. But guess what? I actually went over there."

"So I take it you were drinking rum and smoking Cuban cigars with all the *comandantes*?"

I laughed at the joke, "No, not quite, but I'll have to tell you all about it."

It was Wednesday and we scheduled the barbeque for Saturday. I told him I would ring him up as soon as we left the hotel.

# CHAPTER 25

# Trouble at Disney World

O n Friday, we went to Disney World. It was turning out to be a magnificent trip. Practically a dream come true. A road trip in America with my three siblings, my best friends, and in the summer time. Who could ask for more? We walked and walked through all the long Disney lines and had a blast eating every sort of food you can imagine. Sometime during the evening, I began to have stomach cramps. I thought it was just that normal time of the month, so I decided to take my mind off it and go on all the rides. I went on the boat that drops about a hundred feet in one second and then on the Space roller coaster that totally shakes every inch of your body. A loud speaker announced that the park was not closing at 10:00 p.m., but at 1:00 a.m.! Everyone got so excited we did the rounds on all the rides again.

By one o'clock I could barely walk to the ferry that goes to the parking lot. When I got to the hotel, I took a strong pain killer and went to sleep for a couple of hours. At about four in the morning, I woke up with a terrible stomachache. I threw up a few times, but thought it was food poisoning of some sort. By 7:00 a.m., I was yelling at my brother, "Get me some pain killers! The strongest kind!" We still thought it was food poisoning. At 11:00 a.m., I started repenting of all my sins.

Luisa Fernanda Avila, a Major in the Colombian army

and a close friend of ours, began to read the Bible to me at my request. She had left Colombia immediately after discovering and exposing corruption in the army. Apparently, high-ranking people inside the army headquarters were taking uniforms and selling them to the guerrillas. Since she was in charge of that division, she began to see the inconsistencies and spoke out. Needless to say, her life was in danger, and this road trip with her husband, Alex, was the perfect escape. Alex was also a close friend, one of the producers of the movie, and the actor who did an extraordinary job playing Noel.

This stomachache was the most excruciatingly painful thing I had ever experienced. It felt as if my whole stomach was being stabbed with knives. My brothers could hear me yelling out in pain from my room.

Had we been in Colombia, everyone would have taken me to the emergency room immediately. But we were in the United States, and I didn't have insurance. Why would I think of getting insurance in a country I had never even lived in? We all knew that in any hospital in America, the slightest little test would cost thousands of dollars, and what if it was just something as simple as food poisoning? It was the last thing I wanted to do. I would have preferred to take a direct flight immediately to Bogotá.

Lisa and Sammy arrived. They were completely unaware of the problem since they were staying in a different room. By then it was already 6:00 p.m. As soon as they saw my swollen eyes and yellow skin, they knew I was dying inside.

Alex said, "We need to call Doctor Fernando. Does anyone have his number?"

In less than a minute, we were on the phone talking to Doctor Fernando. After telling him all my symptoms, he replied, "Her appendix has ruptured. You need to take her to the emergency room immediately!"

Nothing like a good old-fashioned doctor who can tell you what is wrong without even having to be there or do any tests. After performing many expensive tests on me, they confirmed Dr. Fernando's diagnosis.

I had never had a hospital experience before. My whole life I had been completely healthy, and anything I did have, God always healed me with no need for outside intervention. When we arrived at the emergency room, the first thing they did was put me in a wheelchair and asked me a few questions. I began to look around and saw that it looked like the lobby of a fancy hotel. It was somewhat comforting to see posters everywhere that said things like, "Don't worry, Jesus will heal you." Or, "Cast your sickness upon Him."

The girl at the front desk asked me, "On a scale from one to ten, one being the lowest pain and ten being the highest, what do you rate your pain as?"

I said, "Five."

Lisa nudged me, "Stop trying to be Mrs. Brave. You are not experiencing five. You were yelling in pain just a few minutes ago! You need to make them feel it's an emergency."

Although perhaps a show would have gotten me in faster in a Colombian hospital, I need not have worried about making a scene in this one. They had me checked out and tested within minutes. Half an hour later, after I had been given three doses of morphine and still felt pain, the lady doctor came into the room. She had a worried expression on her face. "We are not sure what it is, but your whole stomach is inflamed. You will most likely have to be operated on."

Another nurse came in with a receipt and said, "Sorry, but in order to proceed with any other treatments, I am going to have to ask you to pay just 15 percent of what you owe so far, which would come to a little over $2,000."

"Excuse me," Lisa exclaimed, "If that is only 15 percent of

what we owe so far and we've only been here for fifteen minutes, can you imagine how much we'll owe once we get out of here? Alethia, are you well enough to get on a plane tonight for Bogotá and just be treated over there?"

She was asking me, a person who is incapable of turning down a challenge by simply admitting I didn't feel up to it. While slowly trying to get up from the bed, I stupidly said, "I guess I can fly to Bogotá."

All the nurses and the doctor, with grave expressions on their faces said, "Sorry, but we can't let you leave this hospital. You have to stay. Your life is in danger."

My little brother Russell, who in that moment became a man in my eyes, wiped the tears that were beginning to fall down my cheeks and said, "Alethia, God will take care of the bill. Right now, what matters is your life. We're with you. We are going to get through this."

They called my dad and he said, "Just do whatever you have to do to save her life. We'll worry about the money later."

The next day, a Pakistani doctor walked into my room. He showed us the pictures of my stomach, and every part of it was wallowing in yellow puss from the ruptured appendix. With a thick accent, he said, "It is a wonder you are not dead. You are a walking miracle girl. The pictures show that the appendix must have burst at least five days ago, if not more. I don't know how you tolerated so much pain before you came here. Most people would have already died. If we do not operate today, you will die. You are on the edge of a cliff; you haven't gone over, but you will if something is not done."

I had to sign an agreement, and they put me on the operating bed and injected me with something that knocked me out. Before I lost complete consciousness, I remembered the barbeque I had set up with Tom Howes for Saturday. It was now Sunday June 9. I told my brother to call him for me. He didn't answer, but I left a message with probably a really drowsy voice, "Hi Mr. Howes, I'm really sorry I wasn't able to make it to the barbeque yesterday. My appendix burst, and I'm in the hospital going into surgery. I guess I'll see you later."

As I drifted off to sleep I could hear one man nurse say to another, "She looks just like my daughter."

Before I knew it, I was awake in a bedroom with its own TV, a bathroom, and all my friends and family who loved me and were in Orlando surrounding my bed. The nurses were some of the kindest angels God has ever given me. As I could barely get out of bed to get to the bathroom, one black nurse gently scolded me as she was helping me up, "Come on girl, I can do *all* things through Christ who strengthens me!"

I thought, "Yep, that's true; I can even go to the bathroom."

On Tuesday, I received a very pleasant surprise. Tom Howes peeked into my room. I had no clue he was coming or that he knew which hospital I was in. My brother must have given him the information. He sat next to my bed and gave me the most amazing Dove chocolates, but I was not able to enjoy them until after a few months of recovery. We must have talked for hours about everything that was happening on the island with his former captors.

As I look back at his reaction to everything I told him, I realize that if a man who was kidnapped by these people for five and a half years – a person who has every reason to hate them – is open to hearing what God is doing in some of their lives, without having a judgmental attitude, and is not closed to the possibility that perhaps a change in his captors hearts is not so impossible, maybe many more people will also begin to have faith.

After a week of intensive care in the hospital, it was obvious that I was incapable of continuing the 2013 USA *La Montaña* tour or attending the New York Film Academy that summer. I could barely get myself to the bathroom at the pace of a ninety-year-old lady, and I couldn't imagine the thought of walking through the streets of New York with a big heavy camera on my back. The doctors didn't want to let me out of the hospital because my condition seemed to be worsening. I was continually vomiting horrible things.

They repeated all the medical tests. I wrote my friends, "Please pray that the tests will turn out negative because I can't bear to be here one more day." On Friday morning, after six days in "prison," meaning the hospital, I made every effort I could to get out of bed, get washed up, and put on a fake smile I hoped the doctor would find convincing. My doctor walked in and I said with a smile on my face, "I feel so much better today, almost perfect. Please tell me I am free to leave."

He smiled and said, "Your CAT scan and all your other tests came out perfect. You are free to go." I almost hugged him.

My brothers, my sister, and my friends who were on the trip got me a wheelchair and took me out to a restaurant. When the food was served, I almost broke down crying. There are so many things we take for granted. Eating is one of them. The ability to eat was taken from me for a week, and I must have lost many pounds in the process. I asked Sammy to give thanks for the meal, and he told me to do it. I began to pray and my voice cracked. Never before had I felt so much conviction to be grateful. There are so many gifts that God gives us continually that we don't even notice. There is so much for which to be thankful. I was thankful for every friend He had placed by my side during that time. I realized God had blessed me with many amazing people. If anything, the experience taught me to take life a little bit slower, to be grateful for everyone and everything God places in our lives, and not take anything, whether it's your health or the people around you, for granted. I am also thankful my appendix hadn't ruptured a week before in Cuba!

Melissa, my soul sister from Colombia, picked me up and drove me back to Miami and I stayed with her and her family for two weeks. The rest of my friends and family continued their road trip north. I wanted to return to Colombia sooner and bought a ticket, but the airline attendants took one look at me and said I was not capable of flying. Hence, I had to wait in Miami while I recovered a little more. Melissa and her family bathed me in kindness. I have never been treated so well. They were my angels. Doctor Fernando faithfully called me every night to see if I was okay.

I returned to Colombia in the beginning of July, and although the process of recovery took much longer than I had expected it would, I enjoyed every bit of it. I would work only a couple of hours in our home recording studio and then rest. My body couldn't handle more. My cousin Ben would come over and we'd play games or we'd go on a slow walk and eat ice cream, then come home and watch a movie. It was a complete change in lifestyle from what I had just been through. While we were making La Montaña, I forgot the difference between a Sunday and a Monday. Most days, Alex, Lisa, Fercho and I (the four producers) would work eighteen to twenty hours and there came a point where the few hours of sleep I did get would be spent tossing and turning thinking about the different scenes and if they had come out right or if they needed to be improved. Regardless, I had the time of my life. I discovered what it felt like to literally jump out of bed in the morning, excited about the day ahead. Someone once said, "Discover what you love to do and you'll never have to work a day in your life." This couldn't be truer.

One of the greatest, most memorable times was when Kelvin Funkner, our music composer, came down from Canada to help us. For many fun days, my sister Lisa, Kelvin, and me would begin musicalizing the film at 7:00 am and before we knew it, it would be 3:00 am the next day, and we hadn't even noticed because we were having such a blast. This was a project that took several years and when it was finally premiered for the first time, we still did not come to a complete rest. With trailers to make, the soundtrack to mix, the subtitles to insert, the DVD cover to design, the printing, the distribution, the premiers and interviews of the people's reactions all throughout the country, there was little time for anything else but to keep on going. When you love what you do, twenty hours might as well be twenty minutes and we had the time of our lives every step of the way.

I began to wonder, "If this is what it feels like to direct a movie, where it's up to you to make every detail precise and there is little or no rest, I can't imagine what it's like for a president or a general where actual lives are at stake with every decision they make. I don't think they sleep at all!" At least making a movie, no one will die if you make a wrong choice. That thought was comforting. Finally the day came when I was forced to stop. For that, I am thankful.

# CHAPTER 26

# Hugo Tovar

One evening in the middle of July, my mom received a phone call from a Jewish friend of ours named Ernesto Pantevis. Dark skinned, short and plump, the one word I would use to describe Ernesto is authentic. If he doesn't like you, he won't pretend that he does. If he likes you, he will always tell you exactly what he thinks. He is what he is and won't pretend to be anything else. It is refreshing.

"Marina," he said, "I just received a phone call from my lawyer, Hugo Tovar, and he wants Alethia and your whole family to attend the political convention here in Huila that former President Uribe is heading up."

My mom, having voted for him twice and being a great admirer of his work said, "Of course we'll be there! Oh Alethia won't have a problem at all. She'll go and that's final."

When she hung up the phone, I asked, "Where is it that I'm going again?"

She smiled, "Pack your bags 'cause you're going to Uribe's political convention in Huila."

I had met Ernesto Pantevis exactly a year before when I went with my family to premiere our movie in the town of Garzón, Huila. It was hands down the most beautiful drive I had ever been on. Truly, the department of Huila is one of Colombia's best-kept secrets. Since that time I have been there four times, and every trip has been really special. Ernesto had been the one to arrange everything including bathing the town with posters, announcing the event on all the radio stations, and talking the mayor of the town into letting us use the central park for the event. The place was packed with people, and at the end of the presentation everyone gave a loud, heart-felt, minute-long applause.

The day after the presentation, as we were getting ready to drive back to Bogotá, Ernesto's lawyer, Hugo Tovar Marroquín, dropped by the house to greet him. Ernesto introduced us to him, "Alethia, this is my lawyer, Doctor Hugo; he is the one who helped get me out of prison." Then he turned to Hugo and said, "This is Alethia; she just got done making a wonderful movie with her sister about the war in Colombia."

Mr. Tovar immediately said, "I hope the film doesn't trash President Uribe cause I won't have anything to do with it if it does."

"No, it doesn't," I assured him. "Everyone comes out pretty good in it."

He had a point. Many movies made here do a pretty good job of thrashing the army and the country. Lisa and I made every effort possible to not do this, from the writing of the script to the music portrayed throughout the film. When some of the guerrillas on the island asked why the army comes out so well, my dad replied, "It's the army as they should be."

And I always answer, "We portrayed the army as I experienced it during President Uribe's two terms because that is the time period the movie takes place in." I am the kind of person who does not like to get conceptions of things or people based on what I read or on what other people tell me, but on what I experience.

Through those specific years of following my dad deep into the jungles and mountains, we experienced nothing but kindness and a willingness to help us in our peace campaign, from high-ranking generals to the most seemingly insignificant soldiers. Had the events taken place in another president's term, like Pastrana's, Samper's, or Gaviria's, it would have been a different army that had been portrayed in the movie, based on my experience. During their terms, I experienced almost no army in the places we would go, and we lived in constant uncertainty. When we would go out to our farm in Meta, my first question to my dad was always, "Who's in control now? The guerrillas or the paramilitaries?" And the answer would be different each time. The only reason we could go out there is because God had given my dad the grace to make friends with all the different sides of the war.

Sure, the army would come every once in a while, but most of them would destroy the very little we had. Soldiers came to our property and tore the roof off our house and started using the toilets and the bricks of the homes to practice dark, satanic rituals. My mom would warn me not to go out by myself for fear the soldiers might do something to me. And what would they do all day? Swim in the lake with us kids.

Within a few months of the army having been there, the guerrillas attacked, and there was the most terrible blood bath ever. People began to cut up the bodies and throw them in the river. By the time the news channels came to report the tragedy, most of the dead had been cleaned up. Since then, I have never fully trusted a news channel. Had the events of the movie taken place in that time period, the army would have been portrayed a lot differently. I would have been true to what I had experienced.

What I've learned from heading up projects, whether it was a big thing like directing a film with my sister or simply making dinner for my family, is that everything, whether it turns out good or bad, is your responsibility. If something goes wrong, whether it was someone else's mistake or your own, it is your responsibility to make it right again. The good thing is that it is two-sided because everything that goes right can also be attributed to your credit. I think this is the same with presidents. They are in charge, and whether it is a good thing or a bad one, they are the ones responsible for it. If it is a bad thing that happened during their time, then it is up to them to correct it, but we must also give them credit for the things that are done right. What I admired and learned from President Uribe is he always took responsibility for his decisions and always tried to rectify the things that had not gone according to what he had anticipated. That is the mark of a true leader.

Just as we were honest in portraying the army the way we had seen them, we were honest in showing all the other sides as we had experienced them. Had Noel, the guerrilla commander in the film, been a complete terrorist, it would be exactly what we would have shown. But throughout the years, he has been nothing but a good friend to us, and that is what we depicted. Although the movie does not deny the atrocities committed on the different sides of the war, we were careful to portray the individuals the way they had responded to us. Many people get furious because some of the guerrillas and paramilitary men come out good, and they wanted the movie to end with all of the terrorists getting killed, but I was true to what I experienced.

I gave Hugo Tovar a copy of *Rescue the Captors 1*, and he asked me to sign it for him. I wrote, "Thank you so much for getting my friend out of prison."

Ernesto had been falsely accused of being a "pastor who was really a guerrilla." He had been thrown in jail for almost six months. First of all, he was never a pastor. And second, he was never a guerrilla either. His wife, Nenfis, moved heaven and earth until she was finally able to get him out. One of the things she did was hire one of the best lawyers in the country

– Hugo Tovar Marroquín. It was improbable that a lawyer of his stature would help them with their case, but Nenfis was persistent and wouldn't have it any other way. In the end, Hugo realized that the underlying cause of Ernesto's imprisonment had to do with a man who was a racist against Jews and falsely accused Ernesto, as a result. Naturally, he took the case.

Meanwhile, when Ernesto was in prison, God did something incredible there. Ernesto told Hugo, "This is in God's hands. He has shown me the exact date in which I am going to leave this prison. Don't worry about it; just do your job to the best of your ability. But be at rest because God is the one who is going to get me out of here."

Ernesto's complete calm while in prison was something Hugo had probably never seen. Clients would most likely get really upset at him and yell and fight if everything didn't go exactly the way in which they intended, but Ernesto was different. He was dependent upon a completely different being, and as proof, Ernesto was released on the exact date the Lord had shown him.

The day he left, all of his prison mates were sad, but they had found new hope: They had seen God through Ernesto's example. Ernesto and his family had led the way to the beginning of a great friendship with this lawyer. My family and I talked about politics with Hugo and Ernesto for ten minutes, and when the lawyer left the house, Nenfis told me in confidence, "Hugo is good friends with Uribe." By seeing the way he defended him, it wasn't hard to tell.

Politics is something I am not very passionate about, but every once in a while someone comes along who grips my heart. This has happened twice in my life with two different people – one in American politics and the other in Colombian politics. I admire a person who stands his ground no matter what. From the time I was fifteen years old and for eight years, I had the privilege of watching President Álvaro Uribe Vélez in action. I learned a lot about the character traits I wanted to have from watching him. I loved how he stood his ground and maintained his position no matter who he was with. I saw every *cumbre* (summit) all the Latin American presidents would have on live TV, and remember that although he was alone in his positions, he maintained his composure. The few times in which he did lose it were completely necessary and honest.

One thing that impressed me when he was running for the first time was he never disrespected the former presidents. Being a worthy opponent, he treated the other candidates with the utmost respect. In the eight years that I watched him, I was never embarrassed of him as my president because I could always count on an intelligent word coming from his mouth. For the first time in my life, someone made us all believe that perhaps it was possible to have a peaceful country.

The guerrilla commanders in Cuba said the last person they wanted in power again was Uribe. My dad replied, "If it were up to me, I would rather negotiate peace with Uribe. At least with Uribe, you know what you're going to get."

Needless to say, I have always had President Uribe close to my heart and in my prayers. A few months after I met Doctor Hugo, a strong urge to pray for President Uribe overcame me one night. Very seldom do I get a strong inclination to pray for something or someone, but when I do, I know it is significant.

On one occasion, I woke up in the middle of the night and knew I had to pray fervently for my family. They were on a boat trip distributing Bibles and other books along the Ariari River. Later I heard they had been caught in cross-fire between the army and the guerrillas, and in the middle of chaos, their boat had exploded. Valiant soldiers cover-fired for each one of my siblings and parents as one by one they got them out of a gas station at which the guerrillas were firing and into a safer place. Lisa described seeing bullets bounce off the gas tanks. Had one of those bullets penetrated one of those tanks, it could have been the end for my family. Little did I know when I was praying, I was very close to becoming an orphan with not even a sibling left to keep me company.

The same thing happened when I met Noel for the first time. There was a night when I felt such a deep grief for him that all I could do was pray. Now it was happening again with President Uribe, one of the people I esteemed the most. I must have prayed for hours, until a huge burden for him that was in my heart suddenly lifted.

# CHAPTER 27

# President Uribe

Only a couple of days after having had the burden to pray, as I was checking my Facebook news feed, I received a notification saying that the inauguration of Uribe's new book was the very next day. The author would be attending. For years I had dreamt of meeting him, and now at 11:00 p.m., I discovered that at eight o'clock the next morning, he would be signing his book at the Gabriel García Márquez library that was not far from my house. Without even setting an alarm clock, I woke up at 6:30 a.m. and began to get ready. When I walked down the stairs, my brother Russell was up, and I asked him if he wanted to go with me.

"Of course!" He said, "You know, you should give him a copy of *La Montaña.*"

"Why hadn't I thought of that before? Russell, you're brilliant!" I yelled as I ran into the studio and grabbed the only two copies we had left. We rushed out the door and caught a cab for the library. As was expected, the place was full of security guards, and a lady was at the entrance with a huge list in her hands.

"Can you show me your invitation please?" she asked me.

I thought, "Great, they aren't going to let us in." I remembered the Facebook notification and said, "Well, yes, but it came to me through the Internet."

She nodded, "Oh of course, go right in."

A Facebook notification might as well be an Internet invitation. Before going in, I bought a copy of President Uribe's book. In the entrance, a lady was escorting everyone to their seats. She took one look at us and I guess realized we weren't part of the important crowd, so she directed us toward the very back of the auditorium. As I was about to follow her to our seats, to my great surprise, I saw Doctor Hugo Tovar Marroquín standing toward the front of the stage, talking to a senator. He made eye contact with me and motioned me to come toward them. After finishing his conversation, he said, "Come, sit by me." He guided us to the first two rows and took a couple of signs off two chairs that read, "Reserved for Senators and VIP." The lady who had tried to seat me in the back row looked at us from above. All I did was smile at her. Doctor Hugo nudged me and said, "So was it your sister or you, the one who was kidnapped?"

I told him it had been me.

He whispered, "Okay, here he comes. Let me introduce you."

At the other end of the stage was Uribe, greeting a group of people. Precisely in that moment, my brother went out to buy himself a book, and he missed out on the greeting. When the President approached us, Doctor Hugo said, "Mr. President, this is Alethia. She was kidnapped by the FARC."

Doctor Hugo's introduction immediately caught his attention. He wanted to know everything. Suddenly all these questions from the president were being directed at me: "Where were you kidnapped? How long were you held? How old were you?" He was as sharp as I had always imagined he would be.

I passed him a copy of the movie and told him, "The whole story is told in this film if you want to watch it." Although the story of the kidnapping is told in *La Montaña*, since there were so many other stories to tell and so short a time to tell them, Lisa and I decided to keep this episode as brief as possible.

Each second that seemed like an hour in real life is told within a couple of fast-paced minutes.

Years before when I was sixteen, my dad and I had been driving back to our house in the eastern plains when about thirty armed guerrillas surrounded our vehicle in trucks and motorbikes and forced us to go with them deep into a communist, cocaine-growing fortress. For days, the guerrillas held us in a hut, awaiting the final orders of the commander: Would they kill my dad for distributing the book *Marx and Satan*? Or would they let him go? Then one day the guerrillas took my dad with them for his final trial. As I saw him get escorted into a jeep, I wondered if I would ever see him again.

They left me waiting in a little house with a guerrilla girl. In an effort to not get us into any more trouble, this girl had hidden the only copy she had of *Marx and Satan* under a mattress. She gave it to me as soon as they left, and as I read the book thoroughly, I began to realize why they were so upset. With Marx's own writings, the book proves he was never an atheist. Karl Marx was a Satanist. In his poems, he blatantly turns his back on God and sells his soul to the Devil. It is no wonder there is so much darkness among people or nations that follow his teachings.

The author of *Marx and Satan*, Rev. Richard Wurmbrand, was imprisoned for fourteen years during the communist takeover in Romania because he refused to submit to them. They wanted the Christians in the country to support communism, making everyone believe it was exactly the same as Christianity and Jesus was the greatest communist ever. As this convention was taking place and many pastors and priests joined sides with the communist regime, Richard's wife whispered in his ear, "Wipe the shame off of Jesus' face."

He turned to her and said, "If I do, you could lose your husband."

She boldly replied, "I'd rather lose my husband than live with a coward."

In prison they tried to break him of his faith by torturing him and by turning on a loudspeaker all day that repeated over and over, "Communism is good. Christianity is evil." For three years he was placed in solitary confinement in a cell thirty feet underground for refusing to submit to their indoctrination. But even with all of that, the Spirit that was in him was stronger than anything they could do to him and his faith remained unbroken.

As soon as he got out of prison, he went to the United States and started writing and printing books that went directly against everything into which they had tried to brainwash him. *Marx and Satan, An Answer to the Atheists in Moscow* and *In God's Underground* are a few of his many publications.

President Uribe and former Vice President Fransisco Santos spoke for about an hour about the new book, and then it was time for autographs. Immediately a line about a block long was formed. Doctor Hugo motioned for me to follow him, and we passed all the multitudes, the press, the security guards, the red tape and came right to the place where Uribe was calmly giving out signatures. I passed him my copy of his book and to my great delight, when he handed it back to me, it read, "For Alethia, with admiration and gratitude, Álvaro Uribe Veléz."

Now, less than a year later, in August of 2013, we were invited to attend his political convention in the department of Huila. Doctor Hugo was adamant. He had watched the movie and congratulated me on the cinematography, and now he had told Ernesto to tell my mom to tell me he really wanted us to go. The interesting thing was the same thing that happened to me the first time I met President Uribe happened to me now. Only a few days before Ernesto called my mom to tell her about the invitation, I felt a tremendous burden to pray for my favorite former president. As soon as I got done praying, I knew I needed to see him again. I asked God to please open a way if it was truly His will and not just an impulse of mine. Only a few days after the prayer, my mom received the call from Ernesto. I knew it was God's answer to me, and I knew I had to go. My appendix bursting had made it possible to be in the country. Otherwise, I would have been studying in the New York Film Academy, which was what I had planned on doing after finishing the *La Montaña* United States tour. But instead, I had to go back to Colombia for a decent recovery. Despite the difficulties in my health, I was reassured in the fact that no matter what happens, when you are in God's hands and want to follow Him no matter what the cost, He will make sure you are in the right place, at the right time, all the time. Even though you may make mistakes, if your heart is in the right place, He will cover for you.

I called Ernesto and said, "You know what? Since I'm already going over there, I think it'd be nice to show the movie again in Garzón and in La Plata." Ernesto was very enthusiastic about it and immediately started putting movie posters all over the town. My mom, my sister Lisa, Lisa's husband Sammy, and my brother Russell, who had just returned from the tour, drove with our 5.1 theatre surround sound and a huge screen through the most beautiful, lush, green mountains and valleys until we got to our destination. The night before the convention we showed the movie in the town's main square. It was a magical night, and unlike the year before, we actually had copies of the movie to sell after the presentation. Crowds of people wanting free Bibles and their own copy of the film surrounded our car.

The next day as we walked toward the political rally, loud shouts could be heard from afar of: "Uribe! Uribe!" Excitement rang throughout the little town of Garzón, as thousands of people gathered to see their former president. After having to squirm through multitudes, we were finally able to get inside the convention. Since we arrived a little late, there were no chairs left for my family and me. To my surprise, many of the people I had seen at our movie premiere the night before were there, and they were more than happy to share their seats with us, especially since two of the main actors were there – Sammy and Russell. Everyone sang the national anthem, and then the campaign began.

The president had four of his candidates sitting beside him on one side and Hugo Tovar sitting on the other side. My family and I were impressed with Hugo Tovar's performance and felt it was fortunate for the president to have him as a friend and ally. He made clear and concise points and had comprehensible responses to many of the questions the people asked.

At the end of the campaign, the crowds began to leave, and the place was almost empty. My family and I were sitting near the back of the huge auditorium when from the platform, one of Uribe's presidential candidates started walking toward us. It was Óscar Iván Zuluaga, dressed in a humble-looking *ruana* – a classic piece of Colombian attire used mostly by farmers. He greeted each one of us with a handshake and thanked us for coming. Then he walked back to where the other candidates were.

When Hugo Tovar came to greet us, we congratulated him on his performance, and he looked at Sammy and said, "*Don* (a title of respect, similar to Sir) Martin! It's nice to have you here." Sammy laughed and gave him a hug. Sammy had been the one to portray Martin's character (my dad) in the film. Then Hugo said, "I wish I could invite you all to the dinner we're having, but unfortunately I can only invite one person." He looked at me and said, "Alethia, would you like to come?"

In that instant, Ernesto came and said, "Since I helped coordinate the event, I think I can get her name on the list."

Later Ernesto confessed to me, "I'm not much into politics

but a friend's a friend and Hugo helped me get out of prison, so I guess I had to help him getting this convention organized."

A few hours later, I was with Ernesto at the entrance of the fanciest hotel in town. Two guards checked our IDs and sure enough, my name was written down at the end of the list of special guests. We took an elevator to the top floor and found ourselves in a sort of lobby with ritzy rooms with waiters everywhere. A man directed us to the room where the dinner was taking place.

There were three elegant tables set in a U-shape and not more than fifteen people. The table in the front was where President Uribe and three of his four candidates were sitting. Ernesto and I quietly sat down. I couldn't believe I was there, casually having dinner with them. I suppose the people attending were rich folks who owned some of the main businesses of that area, as each of them consulted Uribe and the three candidates regarding their crops and fields and businesses. Ernesto whispered in my ear, "What they're saying is crap. What it costs to fertilize the coffee crops is way too expensive for the farmers to purchase. But since they are the ones selling the product, of course they're telling the president that the prices are just fine."

Being from the city of Bogotá, I had no clue what it cost to maintain a coffee field or fertilize it, but only a few days before, I had talked to a friend of mine in La Plata who owned a coffee farm, and he confirmed the same thing to me. The cost of maintaining and fertilizing his fields exceeded his income, and he had to take another job as a deliveryman to be able pay for the fertilizer he needed. I asked my cousin, whose family also owns a coffee farm, and she said, "To be honest, my dad is very discouraged. What they pay him for his coffee does not cover the cost and the work involved. It's just not profitable for us anymore. What the government needs to do is to make farming profitable again. I'm not saying they need to make us millionaires, but if they protected us and made sure small farmers like us weren't taken advantage of by the big industries, it would motivate us to continue working. But honestly it just isn't what it used to be."

I listened to everyone telling their various problems to President Uribe and his candidates and wondered how many of them were actually being honest. It is hard to tell. Some of them contradicted everything I had actually heard from small farmers who had no reason to lie to me. I wrote Hugo Tovar about it afterwards, and he said I was absolutely right.

It seemed like hours before the dinner ended, and Ernesto and I passed the time whispering our thoughts and opinions to each other. Ernesto said, "I would say it publicly, but I know myself. I would get too heated and riled up and perhaps this is not the right time. Besides, I live in this town. I don't want to make too many enemies."

When the dinner ended, the people who seemed to have been talking for hours got up and swarmed the president. All the presidential candidates left the room as soon as they could, except one. For the second time in one night, Óscar Iván Zuluaga came from the other side of a room to greet me. He shook my hand firmly and then turned around to head out the door. Right then, I remembered I had a few copies of *La Montaña* in my purse. Quickly, before he disappeared out the door, I tapped him on the shoulder. He turned around, and I said, "Here, I just wanted to give you this movie we made."

He took it in his hands, glanced at it and said, "This looks really nice. What part did you play in it?"

"I wrote and directed it with my sister." I replied.

He looked at me and said, "Thank you so much. That's very kind of you." Then he headed out the door.

I thought I wouldn't get a chance to talk to President Uribe since he was in the far end of the room talking to other people.

But instead of leaving the room immediately like others from his delegation had, he walked toward Ernesto and me. He gave me a warm smile and shook my hand. I knew my seconds with him were scarce, so I darted the first question that came to my mind: "Mr. President, did you watch the movie I gave you?"

He looked completely bewildered. Hugo Tovar proclaimed in a loud voice: "President, she is the one that was kidnapped."

Suddenly remembrance filled his face, and I said truthfully, as I pulled another copy of the film out and handed it to him, "I can see you didn't watch the movie I gave you, but I read your book, and never has a book inspired so much patriotism in me."

His reaction to my comment became one of the sweetest memories I have. I can look back at it, and it will always make me smile. He unexpectedly gave me the most heartfelt hug and a kiss on my head, like a father would to his daughter. I smiled at him and continued, "Your book made me laugh. It made me cry. It was excellent." Then I asked him one final question, "Mr. President, is it okay if I take a picture with you?"

With a cheerful attitude he said, "Of course, but with *La Montaña* in it." He grabbed the copy I had just given him and held it up in front of the two of us as Ernesto snapped the picture.

# CHAPTER 28

# Uncle Clayt

The day I arrived home from the convention in Huila, I walked through our recording studio just in time to receive a call from Clayt Sonmore.

Uncle Clayt is a dear friend of my family and one of the people whom I respect the most. He is originally from Minnesota and has been coming to Colombia ever since the 1950s and '60s with a powerful word from God on every occasion. For those who are interested in reading more about him, he has written several books including *Masters of Deception* and *Beware of Strange Fire.*

Uncle Clayt was now approaching the age of ninety and was having difficulties with some of his family members who had a hard time understanding him. A few weeks before calling me, he had wanted to buy himself a nice suit because he felt he needed to look presentable in case he travelled back to Colombia. From decades of experience, he knew that in Latin American countries, the way you look represents the respect you have for the people you visit. In North America, people are more relaxed with their appearance. Some of his family felt that he didn't need to spend their money on a suit especially at his age in life. But, being a very stubborn person, he was adamant. He needed his new suit. Lisa and Sammy sent him a check, and he drove a rental car to a mall to buy some presentable new clothes and to order a fine new suit.

He hadn't told his family before leaving to buy the suit and to make matters worse, his driver's license had already expired. Needless to say, his family was terribly alarmed when he disappeared for several hours. Perhaps in order to make sure this didn't continue to happen, they were looking into sending him to an old people's home, which was the last thing he wanted to do. That is when I received his most desperate phone call.

"Elisha?" An older, croaky voice spoke to me from the other end of the continent. Uncle Clayt had never quite been able to pronounce my name right, and I stopped trying to correct him years ago. I am forever Elisha to him.

"Uncle Clayt! How are you doing? It's nice to hear you.

"I'm not doing very well," he replied. "Elisha, my kids want to put me in an old people's home, and the last thing I want to do is play cards with two old ladies who don't even remember their own names."

Typical Uncle Clayt. He never lacked a sense of humor no matter what situation he was in.

"I'm really sorry about that, Uncle Clayt. You know you are always welcome to stay with us. We'd love to have you."

He said, "Yes, I would surely love that."

An idea came to my mind. "Uncle Clayt, I am going to be speaking up in Fargo, North Dakota, this weekend. How about, you meet me there? We'll fly down to Colombia, and then we can go on to Cuba. God is doing some interesting things over there, and I'm sure the people would love to see you and have you pray for them."

He was ecstatic.

"Okay, I'll meet you in Fargo on Saturday, and then we'll be on our way to Cuba."

Uncle Clayt hadn't been to Cuba for over fifty years. I knew a trip there would be as important for him as it would be for the men and women whom God was beginning to touch. The last time he was there was under completely different circumstances. Like Albert, Uncle Clayt had been part of the Full Gospel Business Men's Fellowship International (FGBMFI). Uncle Clayt was not only a part of the FGBMFI, but he is the only one of the founders who is still alive. For years, Uncle Clayt witnessed tens of thousands of miracles through an outpouring of the Holy Spirit that came right after World War II.

During that time people in America began to desperately seek God, and He began to hear their cries. A huge awakening began where thousands of people would attend a meeting, and by the end, it would be completely full of empty wheelchairs and useless crutches. The blind saw. The deaf heard. God was the God of His people, and He was seeking to have them do things His way.

Uncle Clayt describes it as the "early latter rain." After that, he wrote a book called *Beyond Pentecost*, inspired by God and declaring that there is a place beyond all those miracles; it is called a direct encounter with the Lord of Lords Himself. He said the miracles and visions had left them dry and hungry, and he was looking for something more: God himself.

In the course of that time, the FGBMFI began expanding its meetings all over South America. Members visited Jamaica, Haiti, and many other countries. Countless prophecies were given that came true. One of the many dreams was of a great and final awakening beginning from the most northern tip of South America and flowing down through to the rest of the continent. The country with the tip that is the farthest north is Colombia.

Uncle Clayt knew God had His eyes on Colombia, and that is why he had been coming down throughout the years. He also had a special place in his heart for Cuba, ever since his last trip there in early 1961. The FGBMFI had been doing meetings all across the Caribbean, and he and Demos Shakarian, another founder of the FGBMFI, had landed in Cuba for a few days. On Demos and Clayt's last night on the island, Demos providentially ran into Fidel Castro in the bar of the hotel in which they were staying. They talked for some time as Demos told Fidel about everything God was doing across the United States of America and the Atlantic Ocean. Fidel Castro listened for some time and told Demos he wanted to give the island a chance to see what they had been talking about. He said he would lend them the arena and congregate everyone who wanted to come. They could have meetings where thousands of people could attend.

It was a golden opportunity for the island of Cuba to discover the power of God. As Clayt and Demos discussed how they should go about this new opening, Demos said, "We need to make this as big as we can. We need to go back to the United States and gather all the greatest preachers together and come back in six months to do the meetings."

Clayt felt in his heart that this was wrong. He said, "God is opening the door for us now. We need to do what we can right now with what we have, and God will bless it. If we wait six months – if we even wait only one month, the doors will close." But Demos was not to be convinced. They went back to America and were gathering all the best preachers. But, within a month the Bay of Pigs occurred, and the United States broke relations with Cuba. Soon, Fidel Castro became a diehard communist.

Uncle Clayt says God's people found a glorious paradise in 1948, and it was lost in 1956 because men began putting their own input into the mix. He is one of the only people still alive who can bear witness to the wonderful things that God had begun to do. He also knows what caused it all to end. The church has never been the same since.

Christ used to reign, but now what we see in most places

is anti-Christ. Many people believe the Antichrist is a person who will come in the end and deceive everyone. Although the Greek word *antichrist* is made up of two words *anti* and *Khristos* which mean "anti" and "Christ," *anti* can also mean "in place of." With that second meaning, antichrist becomes "in replacement of Christ." This would mean Christ used to be there at one point, but because His people did not believe and follow Him, because they refused to count the cost and lay down their own plans and ambitions, they received something that replaced Him. This is the sad story that Uncle Clayt constantly tells.

I believe the reason we have received so many faithful visits from him throughout the years is because he knows what went wrong with this great movement, and God has shown him what He wants to do again. He has come down to Colombia because if the prophecy that was told is true and God moves in Colombia like he did in America in the 1940s and '50s, we need to be sure that we do not make the same mistakes that they made, where the glory of God was lost to the point of no return. Uncle Clayt's voice has cried in the wilderness, "Prepare ye the way of the Lord! Make the crooked places straight. Leave your old ways behind and follow the Lord."

Ever since this last encounter with Fidel, Cuba has been like an isolated pancake frying only on one side – the side of communism. For years, I heard that story and it produced sadness in me. I wondered what would have happened on that island had they taken the chance right then and there? But God sees things differently. He sees an opportunity that could have never happened had they not made that mistake because He is capable of using man's failures for His glory.

What happened in the rest of the countries that were visited by God's glory in those days? Shortly after, man's own ways set in, and now the thing that remains to be shown is a whole bunch of empty churches – not empty in people, but empty as far as God's presence is concerned. This is the abomination that causes desolation seen in the Holy Place that Daniel describes. The holy place is the place of gifts and miracles, but it is not the place of the direct presence of God which was called the Holy of Holies in the Bible. To walk in, the priest had to be clean, or he would die. For God to unleash what He has for us in these last days, we must be willing to count the cost – the cost of letting Him wash us clean, strip us from all our filth until the Sun of righteousness rises in us.

My dad tells the story of John Wesley in England. He was an English preacher whom God used to transform his country. History books don't tell it right, just as they don't tell how the west was truly won. No one tells about the great awakenings in America and England that caused them to become truly great nations. The Wild West in the United States was not won with cowboys. It was won with men and women who were on fire for God. They would walk or ride with Bibles in their backpacks for hours through snow and desert to get the Word of God out to the people until those wild woods became a flaming fire burning with the life of God.

England was won over by men like John Wesley who started reading the Bible for the first time in their own language. John Wesley preached in the churches until one day they kicked him out. But that didn't stop him. He went to his father's grave and preached standing on top of it. He preached at the top of his lungs to the multitudes that gathered around him: "I know I don't live in victory now, but here it says that in Him there is victory! And I will continue preaching until I have that victory, and God's life becomes alive in me." By the end of his life, more people would crowd around to see him walk by than when the king passed by.

John Wesley had three points. One was that anyone could

be saved. Up until then, it was thought that only a select and fortunate few could be saved by God. The second point was if you are saved, you will know it. Most people thought God had determined beforehand who would be saved and who wouldn't and there was no way of knowing. The third point was if you are saved, you will show it.

Now, because of God's people doing things man's way, Cuba lost a tremendous opportunity, and for fifty plus years has lived in darkness. However, I remember something a friend once told me. She said that counterfeit light will always be the greatest darkness. More darkness can be felt in a church that once had God's presence but lost it because God's people didn't follow Him with all their hearts.

Likewise, more darkness can be felt in a country that used to have God's presence and blessing but has lost it, due to counterfeit light clothing itself as truth, than a country that never had God's presence. I have felt more darkness travelling across North America than in going into a dark island. Cuba never had the real light. Cuba's darkness is just darkness; it is not pretending to be something it's not. This makes Cuba a golden opportunity right now. It's like a pancake that needs to be turned over, and it can be done with one strike.

I knew it was historic that I was going back to the island with Uncle Clayt after everything that had happened, after all the history and after more than fifty years of reaping the consequences of a missed opportunity. It may be that no one records it in history books, but it might be one of those many events that changes the course of entire nations.

I went to Fargo, North Dakota, to fulfill my speaking engagement, and during the middle of the day, Clayt arrived at the event with a longtime friend of my dad's, David Cutsforth, and his wife. David and my dad are from the same town of Grand Rapids, Minnesota. Uncle Clayt gave me a great big hug. I was as happy to see him as he was to see me. In that moment as we sat down and discussed what we were going to do next, neither one of us could have imagined that in less than three days, we would all be sitting in Cuba.

Clayt and I began planning. We knew our mission was to get to Cuba. David Cutsforth was skeptical about the whole plan at first, but Clayt was stubborn as ever. We were going to Cuba and that was final.

We had trouble getting Clayt's documents in such short notice. We were in Fargo, North Dakota, and his passport was all the way in Colorado and he needed it immediately. After discussing several options, we finally came to a solution. Clayt would fly to Colorado that day to regain his passport. Then he would fly directly to Colombia the next day. It is fortunate he has a son who is a pilot and gives him free tickets everywhere. I would continue with business as usual at the convention and fly home as soon as I finished the next day. David would meet us there on Monday. It was Saturday, and in less than a day, Clayt needed to get his passport, fly to Bogotá and then to Cuba on Tuesday. It was going to be tight, but we could make it. Immediately after coming up with the plan, we drove Clayt to the airport and got him on the first flight out.

On Tuesday, Clayt Sonmore, David Cutsforth, my dad, my two brothers, Steve Salisbury (the American reporter), Luis Humberto Montejo, the former governor of Boyacá, and I were all miraculously on a flight to Havana.

# CHAPTER 29

# Clayt Sonmore in Cuba

It is one thing to travel to Cuba alone and quite another experience when you are pushing an older man in a wheelchair. We went through immigration and security without difficulty. Everyone was in their kindest behavior. We were stopped only once on our way out by two officers, a lady and a man. Among the food I had in my suitcase, they found some popcorn – an illegal seed.

The lady said, "I'm really sorry; it's illegal to bring seeds into the country. I can't let you take this through." But then she looked at Clayt who was in his wheelchair, and she exclaimed full of compassion, "Oh no! Is this food for the poor old man?"

"Yes," I said.

As she looked at him with empathy, she cried out, "How could I take away the poor old man's food? I can't! Just leave with the seeds, but know that it's illegal, okay?" And off we went with all our popcorn.

We stayed at the same place we had stayed before – the cement house that overlooked the ocean with a beautiful view of Havana in the distance. Since it was now summer, my dad, brothers, and I would have the most delicious midnight swims in the warm water as we contemplated the stars above and the city beyond. My dad told my youngest brother Dylan, who was thirteen at that time, to be careful of how he spoke of the island while we were there because anyone could be listening. From then on whenever we had anything secret to say, Dylan would comically look around him and say in imitation of Steve Martin in *The Pink Panther*, "The Wveather is vreally nice."

Now these guerrilla guys from the delegation are not that easy to connect with. On the previous occasions, they had sent their guys to check us out for a few days before meeting with us. This time it was different. The morning after we got there, Ivan Márquez woke up from his sleep with a revelation given to him. He saw a vision where the heavens opened up and a Voice said that today he was going to receive revelation and understanding. He knew the first thing he needed to do was head for our house. To our great surprise, Ivan, Santrich, Noel, Yuri, and Maritza all arrived early that morning. As soon as they reached the privacy of the deck that overlooked the ocean, Ivan exclaimed, "The coast is clear. Please pray for us!"

My dad translated as Uncle Clayt prayed for each one of them, beginning with Ivan. It is amazing what prayer can do for someone. In some cases it blinds the person, as it blinded President Santos when he allowed the Kogi Indians to lay hands on him. In other cases, when it is a true representative from God who prays for you, it can open up your eyes and set you into a higher place in Him.

I am reminded of another occasion in which something very interesting happened with Albert and Luis Humberto. Luis Humberto asked Albert to pray for his cousin, who is President Santos. Albert laid hands on Luis Humberto and prayed for him as if he was the president himself. He asked God to clear up his understanding and to rid him of all blindness.

His prayer gave me an idea. One of my cousins had always suffered from seizures. So I came up to Albert and asked him to pray for my brain as if I was her. Some time later when I was visiting my grandma, without foreknowledge, she told me my cousin had stopped taking her seizure medication because the Lord had healed her. When my grandma told me the period in which this had happened, it turned out it was at around the same time that Albert had prayed for her through me! I don't know the effect of the prayer Albert prayed for Luis Humberto's cousin, but it was incredible to hear what happened to my cousin as a result.

When Clayt finished praying for them, Ivan said he wanted to make a national day of contrition for all the wrongs they had committed. He said, "I feel in my heart that we must do this, but I don't know when. It is necessary to do this as a country for all the wrongs we have committed. And not only us, but many others need to do this for all the damage they did as well. Then a new day can begin."

Santrich, who was sitting nearby, asked me, "You know that song you sent me, Alethia?"

"Which one? 'Amazing Grace'?"

He said, "Yes, that's the one. I heard it and I read the story you wrote me of the blind man who composed it. I really liked the song and the man's story. Thank you."

I had sent him a beautiful masterpiece of "Amazing Grace" played on the piano and the violin with the lyrics translated into Spanish and a synopsis of the man who had written it. John Newton, the composer, was an English slave trader for many years until God found him. The lyrics to his song talk about redemption and forgiveness no matter what the past sins had been.

I wrote to Santrich and told him, "This man had his slaves in the most inhumane conditions, stacked one on top of the other to the point where they had to pee on each other. One day God found him and set him free. After a while, he renounced slavery and never practiced it again. The ironic thing about this song is when he was trafficking the black slaves, he could see just fine. However, when he became older, his eyes grew dim and he became blind, yet that was when he saw God. So he writes, 'I once was blind, but now I see.' Even though he had been able to see, he was blind, because he couldn't see God. He knew that all his sins had been forgiven and forgotten, and he had been redeemed."

> *Amazing Grace, How sweet the sound*
> *That saved a wretch like me.*
> *I once was lost but now I am found*
> *Was blind, but now I see.*
>
> *'Twas grace that taught my heart to fear.*
> *And grace my fears relieved.*
> *How precious did that grace appear*
> *The hour I first believed.*
>
> *When we've been there 10,000 years*
> *Bright shining as the sun,*
> *We've no less days to sing God's praise*
> *Than when we first begun.*

After Santrich and I hummed the song a little, he said, "You know, Alethia, you probably saw the video about me, the one where I appear singing, "*Quizas, Quizas, Quizas...?*"

I said, "Yes, I did see it."

Of course I had seen it. The whole country had. It was a horrible video in which a reporter asked him and Ivan if they were going to ask their victims for forgiveness. Instead of answering, Santrich began to sing a well-known song called "*Quizas, Quizas, Quizas,*" meaning, "Perhaps, Perhaps, Perhaps." When the country watched it, it seemed like the most indecent mockery of all the war's victims. Anyone who had hated the guerrillas before detested them now.

Santrich continued, "I want you to know that when they edited the video, they changed the audio of the question. That really wasn't what they had asked me. What happened was that the reporter had been urging me to answer the question: 'Are you going to apologize to the government?' He didn't ask me about the war's victims; he asked us about the government. It was about the fifth time he asked, and I didn't want to be rude so I just sang that song. When the video came out, they had inserted a different question. It would be horrible if I were that insensitive toward the war's victims. How could anyone believe that?"

My heart sank a little, "I'm really sorry about that." I said, "I believe you." Working in video, I know how easy it is to manipulate and distort information. Inserting a different audio to the question would have been extremely easy, and anyone who hates them would have done it. It is amazing how much the media does to distort things one way or another depending on their political agenda. People can change; extraordinary things can happen; God can intervene. Yet it will never appear in an article.

Only the news that covers everyone hating each other and people being completely insensitive makes it into the headlines. The rest doesn't matter. Maybe the rest just doesn't sell. But if Colombia, or any country for that matter, wants a new beginning, we must stop listening to those who tell us who to hate and only listen to the One who told us to love our neighbor as ourselves and pray for those who curse us. It may be true that someone is the worst human being ever, but they will never be able to change if someone doesn't have hope for them.

Albert told me of a lieutenant who had faith in him and how it completely changed his life. That faith was all it took for him to become a changed person.

This happened to me years before when I was in Minnesota.

I was going through a desperate time in my life. I had lost hope and was in despair regarding the disgusting darkness in those who claimed to be the people of God. On a cold, rainy night, I called Uncle Clayt at two o'clock in the morning. I was crying and he prayed for me. He didn't pray that the situation around me would change but rather that I would have peace and joy and love. As soon as I hung up, the Lord Himself met me in that little cabin, and I discovered God Himself. He gave me true joy and hope and told me He was going to win over this darkness that covered His people. That was all I needed to know. He gave me a way out of the hopeless situation where there seemed to be no way.

Likewise, Colombia is in a predicament that seems to have no way out. Most of the countries surrounding us want to impose themselves on us. Although it has been close to happening many times, God has had mercy on this country and has not let us fall into the hands of our enemies. The nation of Israel is also surrounded by enemies and seems to be alone in all its battles.

Before the former President of Venezuela, Hugo Chavez, died of colon cancer, he stated with hatred in his eyes that he cursed the nation of Israel from the depths of his bowels. He would openly proclaim that Colombia was the Israel of Latin America.

It is true that Colombia is the Israel of Latin America in the sense that all our neighbors have turned their backs on us and have become our enemies. We are standing alone fighting for our sovereignty, with the exception of the United States. God has allowed this to happen, (even the weakening of the United States) so the nation of Colombia would learn to depend on Him, just as Israel had to do in the times of the Bible.

God did not change the circumstances surrounding me when I was in trouble; He changed me. He gave me the ability to win. He may not change the circumstances surrounding

Colombia, but He can give us the possibility of winning. In the Bible, in order for Israel to win against their enemies they had to turn to God. God always provided a way out even when there seemed to be no way, and in the end Israel's enemies became afraid of them.

Now things in Colombia were happening differently from what everyone had anticipated. Perhaps, in the Devil's great scheme to conquer Colombia, he thought that by blinding the president into doing this peace plan, he would destroy the sovereignty of our country in one final blow. What he probably didn't take into consideration was the possibility that some of these men would begin to turn to God, and the dark fortress would begin to emanate light. God has a hidden agenda. Clayt and Albert coming to the island of Cuba were not in the Devil's plans. My dad encountering God during his kidnapping was not in his plans. No, the Devil had a myopic view of what was going to happen. God has the full vision, and He is using us as part of His masterpiece. God can use everything the enemy does to get us to depend more on Him, and this has pushed Colombia into a deeper dependence on God: we realize that nothing else will do.

Later that day, Ivan and his comrades took us out for lunch to one of the most exquisite restaurants in Cuba. Even Steven Spielberg had eaten there. We sat around a table that looked like it had been taken from the Renaissance age. An old wooden piano stood in the back, and the whole room was decorated with golden and pink antiques. This met Uncle Clayt's expectations, because he had owned one of the finest restaurants in the Twin Cities when he was younger. Plus he looked like he fit right into the assemblage of people that had been there with his sharp new suit.

The waiters served us the most delicious meats, pork, vegetables, rice, and beans. I randomly chose my seat, and to my surprise Ivan Márquez and Luis Humberto Montejo sat in front of me. Luis Humberto had gone to the island on a previous occasion with my dad and became good friends with Ivan. They were like two peas in a pod.

He had also met Rodrigo Granda that time (another guerrilla leader), and it was fortunate that when Luis Humberto was governor of Boyacá and Rodrigo Granda had been thrown into the maximum security penitentiary, Luis Humberto had treated him very kindly. He had been sentenced to 500 years, and somehow at the request of the French President Sarkozy, Granda had been released and had made his way to Cuba. Granda never forgot the love and kindness shown to him by Luis Humberto, and this resulted in Luis being trusted by them. Later, Granda told my dad that after his miraculous release from prison he came to believe in God too.

Now, I could see that Luis and Ivan were speaking to each other in hushed tones. Ivan whispered to Luis, "Pablo Catatumbo wants to meet with you today. Are you willing to talk to him?"

There are seven members of the FARC secretariat who make all the big decisions. Three of them were on the island – Ivan Márquez, Rodrigo Granda, and Pablo Catatumbo.

Luis Humberto replied, "I'm willing to talk to him but with one condition."

"What would that be?" Ivan asked.

Luis Humberto looked across the table to me and to my astonishment, he said, "I will go only if Alethia goes."

Ivan looked at me and nodded his head in approval, "I'm sure that wouldn't be a problem. I'll send a car for both of you at around 4:00 p.m."

# CHAPTER 30

# The Voice of God

At four o'clock sharp, a black Mercedes pulled up to our house and drove us through the best neighborhoods in Havana until we arrived at a gated community called "El Laguito," where exotic mansions surrounded a lake and wooden walkways adorned a small forest. The car parked in front of one of the nicest, stone walled houses, and Luis Humberto and I got out of the car and rang the huge doorbell.

Out came Santrich, Ivan, Yuri, and Maritza to greet us with warm friendly smiles. They invited us into the house, and we bumped into Pablo Catatumbo in the hallway. He appeared to be in his fifties and gave Luis Humberto and me each a big welcoming hug.

Luis Humberto and I sat about a meter and a half across from Pablo Catatumbo and Ivan Márquez in the large, impersonal, white living room. Yuri sat diagonally to us. Ivan Márquez introduced me as the director of *La Montaña* and said that he had loved the cinematography. Pablo said, "Yes, I saw it, but there are certain issues we need to address concerning that movie." And then he added in a gruffer tone, "But we did not come here to talk about *La Montaña*."

Pablo told us of certain encounters they had with Pablo Escobar on military bases. He asked me one peculiar question, "Alethia, since you are a journalist, figure this one out.

People think this is a war of light against darkness, but you see it isn't always like this. See if you can find the answer to this question: How did Pablo Escobar get his elephants from Africa to Colombia?"

It was a seemingly random question to which I still do not know the answer. He seemed confident in what he was doing and very confident in what he spoke of. He blatantly continued, "Some people may have humanitarian reasons for why they see kidnapping as something wrong."

In the meantime, I noticed Ivan's face of uncertainty. I knew he was going through an extreme, internal battle. Finally, the diplomat in him came out and said, "Pablo, let Alethia tell you about Clayt Sonmore. He is a very interesting man from the United States, and he gave me a book he wrote called *Masters of Deception*. It's in English, but we can have someone translate it for us."

"Ah, very interesting, tell us about this Clayt man, Alethia." Pablo courteously said.

The spotlight was on me, and I began to tell the story from the very beginning, skipping no details.

"In 1948, Clayt and his wife, Jeanne, were planning to go to Colombia as missionaries, but due to some business issues, Clayt decided to wait a few months before going. His best friend, Roland Krefting, with his wife and children went on ahead to work as the chief engineer in the mines of Zipaquirá and do missionary work in his spare time. Only a few weeks after they arrived, Roland Krefting was brutally tied by the ankles to the back of a car with rope from the Catholic priests and dragged down the street. His small children and wife wailed as they helplessly saw their father and husband die.

"At that time, Catholics dominated the entire country, and there was little or no tolerance for any other faith. It is reported that over a third of protestant Christians were killed, although the Catholics never received any of the blame. History books state the bloodshed was the result of a war between two political parties and the surge of the communists."

Pablo Catatumbo nodded his head in deep thought. "There may be some truth to what you're saying," he said.

I continued on with my story. "Uncle Clayt made sure to tell it to me many times growing up, and I never forgot it.

"Roland Krefting's body lay completely disfigured and unrecognizable. They sent what could be salvaged in a coffin all the way to Minnesota. When Uncle Clayt and his wife attended his funeral, they placed their hands on the coffin and wept, asking God to send a hundred more missionaries to Colombia who would replace their dear friend Roland. God decided to send Uncle Clayt and his wife, and ever since then they have been coming frequently. Uncle Clayt says that when he first started coming, Catholics outside the buildings where he spoke would angrily throw stones at the windows in an effort to make him stop preaching. But his stubbornness and the confidence he had in God enabled him to continue. A defining point in Colombia's history was when Clayt spoke to members of the parliament in February 1967.

"God gave him the words in power, and by the end of his speech, every member was weeping. Clayt said, 'Though Simon Bolivar (the George Washington of Latin America) had liberated you in 1819 from the brutal slavery that had been imposed on you by Spain, your country shortly thereafter sold its birthright of freedom to another slavery, more brutal, crushing, and demonic than the former. This crushing foreign power is none other than the Roman Catholic Church – ever since Colombia signed a Concordat with Roman Catholicism and its Pope. This selling of your birthright was nearly 150 years ago. Rome thrives and keeps its captives only where poverty and illiteracy exist.

"'Everywhere the chains of Catholicism have been broken,

that nation or peoples were immediately released from that spirit, and their poverty and illiteracy have been significantly reversed. God's displeasure with this foreign power will bring sure judgment upon this nation where a third of the population will die unless you repent of this unholy alliance, break the Concordat with Rome, and free your people.' He closed with these final words, 'You will soon know that what I have spoken today is the word of the Lord when a sign of the coming judgment, not the judgment itself, soon comes as an earthquake that will shake every square foot of your nation.'[1]

"Uncle Clayt got on a plane, and an hour after he arrived back in Minneapolis, he turned on the radio. The top news report was that an earthquake had shaken every square corner in Colombia, knocking down most of the steeples and the pagan statues of the saints and of the virgin and the crucified Christ. My dad says false religion always wants to represent the Lord Jesus either as a helpless baby or as a dead person stuck on a pagan symbol. But they never paint the real picture – the picture of Him seated on the throne with his Father, resurrected in new life with all power and glory to fulfill his will in us. This earthquake took place exactly twenty-four hours after he had spoken to parliament. It even reached the island of San Andrés, which is closer to Nicaragua than to Colombia, but it still belongs to Colombia.

"The word of the Lord that has come many times through prophets like Clayt Sonmore is that 'God is going to break the back of Catholicism in Latin America, beginning in Colombia.'"

Ivan, Pablo, and Luis Humberto listened attentively to my story when suddenly Rodrigo Granda, the other member of the secretariat, walked in. I had never met him before, but he gave me a huge hug and said he was at our service. He left and we continued talking. I said, "There is more to it in 'Masters of Deception,' the book Clayt gave you."

---

1    Taken from the book *Beyond Pentecost*, written by Clayt Sonmore.

Then they began discussing political issues with Luis Humberto, and shortly after, Pablo Catatumbo asked to be excused because he had to attend another meeting. Then Santrich, the blind guerrilla leader, walked in and sat next to us, and we began a more casual and informal conversation with Ivan, Yuri, Santrich, and Luis Humberto. They were all relaxed, smoking big, fat Cuban cigars as I ate a slice of delicious lemon pie. Suddenly amidst the laughter and the jokes, Ivan said coolly to us as he puffed smoke from his mouth, "One thing we need to understand is that the voice of the people is the voice of God."

Then everyone, save me and Luis Humberto, began laughing and continued on in the careless chatter. Everything in my body began to churn. I knew my dad had had a conversation with them before when he clearly told them that the voice of the people was not the voice of God because man is corrupt. But obviously, it hadn't hit home. I don't know what came upon me. Usually I am not affected with people's political or religious opinions regarding things, but in this case, since it was God himself they were talking about, I knew I had to defend His name. I just didn't know when. And since everyone continued talking, there really wasn't a moment.

I prayed God would give me a right moment. But, sometimes there is never a right time to state a truth. It was like in *The Silver Chair* by C. S. Lewis when the witch was soothing Puddleglum, Jill, and Eustace into her dark spell and telling them that Aslan, the Lion who represented God, did not exist. There wasn't a right moment to stop her, but Puddleglum simply stuck his foot in the fire, and the spell was broken. The children woke up to their reality.

I interrupted whatever it was they were talking about and said, "Excuse me Don Ivan, but I disagree with you. The voice of the people is not the voice of God."

The air stiffened. Suddenly, as if I had touched a very sacred cow no one dared touch, they all started refuting me. I began to defend my point, but amidst so many other voices that came toward me, my voice could barely be heard. They were firmly stating their opinions on why they thought the voice of the people was the voice of God. Ivan puffed his cigar a few times and said, "You can't be so radical, Alethia!"

In that moment I believe God gave me the authority to speak and all the inspiration I needed. I exclaimed, "On this point I will be very radical, Don Ivan." Everyone who had been chattering and discussing their points of view remained completely silent.

I continued with just as much force, "The voice of the people will never be the voice of God because the people may love you today, but tomorrow they might decide to hate you. But God is consistent; God will love you today; He will love you tomorrow, and He will love you the day after tomorrow." Ivan's undivided attention was on me so I persisted, "He doesn't change. But people are fickle and they are corrupt. Ever since Adam and Eve disobeyed God, people are fallen. Why do you think my dad and I, and so many others persevered to go into dangerous war zones and come here to talk to you? It's because we love you. It's because we know God loves you, and we want to see Him change you. And you won't believe what I'm about to say, but…"

Ivan interrupted me and said, "Of course I believe you!"

So I continued, "You won't believe this, but there are people all over the world in Australia, Canada, the United States, Finland, and New Zealand who also love you and pray for you and want to see Colombia transformed, beginning with all of you."

Luis Humberto told me later that he was praying for me all the while, so God would give me the right words to say.

Whatever darkness was in the air before I said this receded, and a new atmosphere emerged. Santrich said, "Oh, I guess I was confused. I thought God could talk through crowds, but I guess that isn't so."

I turned to him and said, "One day, when we all enter into His glory, He will be able to talk through crowds because they will all be in tune with Him. But for now, He only talks through individuals who have allowed Him to clean their hearts."

The night became calm and the air felt fresh. Now, in a completely different attitude and as the hosts to their special guests, Ivan and Santrich took us on an elaborate tour of their house. They showed us their bedrooms and their most prized cigars and belongings. Santrich showed me his paintings and his instruments. He played the saxophone and insisted that I play, so I tried to the best of my memory. I hadn't played for more than five years. Then he produced a sort of Indian flute and played it as I've never heard anyone play before. When he was done, he handed it over to me and said, "Here. I want you to have it. The next time I see you, you can play me a song."

After we went back downstairs, Santrich withdrew to his room. When he returned, he had two beautifully painted birds on two separate tiles. He gave one to me and one to Luis Humberto. I rose to thank him, and my foot knocked over his glass cup and caused a huge mess. He graciously smiled and told me not to worry about it and that accidents like that happened all the time. Then Ivan looked at us and at Maritza, Yuri, and Santrich and said he wanted to go for a walk.

The evening had taken an unlikely turn. Instead of discussing politics or religion, we were treated as guests in the house of a few old friends who showed us their best hospitality and did not want us to leave. We walked around the lake and through the forest until it became dark and talked about everyday things such as travelling, exercise, the beauty of the other houses, the bike Luis Humberto had given Ivan, music, and the different cultures. It was the kind of talk you would have with friends you feel comfortable with. Then at around ten o'clock, they called Ernesto, our Cuban friend, and asked him to pick us up.

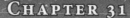

# CHAPTER 31

# Forgiveness

T he next few days in Cuba were filled with fun and joy. Luis Humberto had a barbeque for the FARC delegation, and they all came over to eat meat and share with us. My dad, Ivan, and my brothers talked as they viewed the ocean and ate. Ivan told me with a twinkle in his eyes as he patted my dad on his back as an old friend would, "Alethia, if you ever want to get your dad to stop talking about religion, get him to talk about airplanes." My brothers and I all laughed, knowing how true the statement was. Suddenly it started raining, and the twenty plus people who were at the house scattered for cover.

As everybody parted, we ended up in separate rooms. I found myself in one of the living rooms with Santrich and David Cutsforth, my dad's good old Minnesotan friend. David, who is accustomed to meetings in America where everyone sits down and one person preaches, had wanted to do the same thing on the island. But, it seemed an impossible thing to do. He whispered in my ear and asked about gathering everyone together because he had something to say he felt was from God. I whispered back, "Just take the opportunities God gives you. We can't make big meetings here. If you find yourself with only one guy, maybe the message is just meant for him. Go ahead and speak what's in your heart. I will translate for you."

David Cutsforth began to tell Santrich about forgiveness. He said in order for Colombia, or any person, to progress in what God had for them, it was necessary for them to forgive and be forgiven. He said forgiveness had nothing to do with what other people were doing or whether or not they were even asking for forgiveness. To ask for forgiveness and to be forgiven were decisions everyone had to make despite what others were doing.

He said, "When you ask for forgiveness, don't think that the government must do so before you do or give any kind of conditions. First of all, you should ask for forgiveness without caring who else does. Second, you should place no conditions on your repenting. This is something God requires of you. If you trust Him, He will take care of the rest of the people."

Santrich nodded his head in approval. David continued, "And when God grants you that forgiveness, no one can take it from you. When He says you are free, you are free indeed, and that is priceless."

Next, they listened to the gospel country style music David, an expert musician, had on his iPod. Santrich, also being an expert musician, thoroughly enjoyed the free lesson in American gospel music.

That night, Ernesto came over to our house because he was worried about his wife. Albert had prayed for her unborn baby four months before so that it wouldn't be born prematurely. Now the opposite problem was happening. The baby was a week overdue, and there was no sign that it wanted to come. She was going to have to go to the hospital and get induced if the baby wasn't born that day.

I told Ernesto to have her come over for Clayt to pray for her, and about twenty minutes later she arrived – big and pregnant and eager to be prayed for. Uncle Clayt laid his hands over her belly, blessed the child, and asked God to open her womb up so the baby would be born that day. Not more than a few hours later, Ernesto arrived at our house, happy because his baby girl had been born. There had been no need of a medical intervention.

My dad and I stayed up talking every night about everything that was happening and the extraordinary and unlikely way in which God was working. I like watching my dad think and asking him what is on his mind because it is always interesting. As we had something to drink and contemplated the ocean, the stars, and the city lights beyond, I asked my dad what he had on his mind, and he said, "You know what I'm thinking? This baby was conceived at about the time when Noel first contacted us to come to the island. Then, it almost died and Albert had to pray and it lived. Now, at the end of the nine months, it didn't want to be born, and Clayt had to pray the little girl into being again. I think that whatever God conceived here with these guys on the island is going to be brought to life. Albert and Clayt have been used of God to give them a little push in the right direction."

Before leaving, I showed Noel the pictures of me with President Uribe and said, "Noel, what do you think of making Uribe part of your Friendship Plan?"

Noel looked at the picture and solemnly nodded his head in approval. "Yes," he said.

I knew it was hard for him. President Uribe had been one of the people who had caused them the most harm. "Well, you can start by praying for him." I said.

Noel looked up at me after analyzing the picture a long time and smiled, "So Uribe has seen *La Montaña*?"

I replied, "I gave it to him. He's a busy man; who knows if he's seen it?"

Later I wrote Ivan, Santrich, Yuri, and Noel and told them that just as Albert had prayed for them, he was also praying for Uribe. That was probably one of the reasons he was still alive after so many attempts to kill him. Prayer is also the likely reason Noel and the others were also still alive, because so many people had intervened for them in prayer.

# CHAPTER 32

# Albert Returns

In November 2013, Albert came to visit us once again. Something special always happens on his visits. On this occasion, we were a hundred kilometers south of Cali, Colombia, praying for the Indians in that region. The Indian leaders had set up a day for Albert to speak and to pray for them. Bus after colorful bus (they call their typical busses *Chivas*, or Goats) full of Indians filled the parking lot, and the place was packed with about 2000 people. The leaders of that church service began to ask people for money and for anything they had: chains, watches, rings etc. That was short-circuited when Albert got up to pray. My dad introduced him by saying that one thing that distinguished Albert from the rest of the people who had similar gifts was that he never charged a penny for using his gift to heal people.

A terrible thunderstorm cut off the electricity and almost blew Albert off the platform. The Indian leaders helped Albert off, and he began to pray for people while the electric power was being restored. Many were healed of cancer. A guerrilla commander, who was watching the proceedings from the sidelines got called up to the front by my dad. He had been injured in a bomb blast and had one leg that was twisted and crippled, and almost four inches shorter than the other. My dad sat him down in a chair and asked Albert to pray for him. The crippled leg straightened out and then, to the commanders' absolute surprise, grew longer than his good leg! The look on the guy's face was priceless. Albert smiled at this and said the bad leg was out of joint. He prayed again and the leg snapped back into place, equal in length with the other.

Albert celebrated his eighty-eighth birthday at this gathering, and the Indians went wild congratulating him and giving him presents. Unlike what I have seen in North America, the Indians, Colombians, and Cubans all highly respect and venerate old age.

Albert visited three different Indian groups and prayed for a multitude in that weekend alone. He was scheduled to fly out on Thursday night from Cali, but on Tuesday my hairdresser, Mirian Ariza, a sweet Christian friend, called and said that she had finally convinced her cousin's husband, Carlos Garzón, an agnostic who works for President Santos and has access to all the prisons in the country, to let us into the maximum security prison in Bogotá. I had told her about Albert and his healing ministry, and she moved heaven and earth to get Carlos to let us into the prison. Albert had been praying for every side of the conflict except the paramilitary, and this prison was full of former paramilitary leaders who had surrendered after the true events of the film *La Montaña*. These were the real characters portrayed in that movie, now doing their time in jail. When I heard we had access to finally pray for these prisoners, I didn't hesitate to buy Albert and my dad tickets to leave Cali on Wednesday afternoon.

In Bogotá, Albert prayed for many friends and family members at our home. He spoke of forgiveness and how it was necessary to forgive our parents because in many cases they were also victims of their own parents. He said that in order to receive God's blessing, it was necessary to honor our father and mother no matter what.

About twelve people were prayed for in our small living room. While these miracles were taking place, the very hard-to-get Carlos, the presidential guy, was chatting away on his cell phone, not taking any notice of what was happening. As he and Miriam were on their way out, my dad asked him if he wanted Albert to pray for him. Carlos nodded in a get-me-out-of-here way. Albert sat him down on a chair. He measured both legs and one was shorter than the other one. The discrepancy was healed. Then Albert prayed for his knee that was bent due to a bomb that had exploded near him when he was a police lieutenant. It straightened out completely. When this happened, Carlos could not believe it. His eyes got really big, and he said the pain was gone, and he had felt a warm sensation on his knee while Albert was praying. I don't think he knew what had hit him. Then Albert told Carlos to stand at attention, and his back, which had also been hurt in the bomb blast, snapped back into place perfectly.

The next day my dad, Albert, and I went to meet up with Carlos in the maximum security prison. The prison was not as bad as I thought it would be, as it included a church, a garden, a basketball/soccer court, and three stories of rooms. I dreaded the possibility of seeing people being treated like animals. This was not the case with the paramilitary men who had surrendered to the government. It would defeat the purpose of being in prison if they had been in a five-star hotel, but they were being treated like human beings.

When the paramilitary men saw us come in, they all gathered in a small room to hear Albert and my dad speak. Albert told of his time in the army and how he could relate to their hard shell as a result. He said that in the army a hard shell develops, and it is impossible to get rid of it without the power of the Lord Jesus. Albert asked me to tell of the miracles I had seen that week, so I gave them a report on what had happened.

Surprisingly, Carlos spoke up and told the story of how the Lord had healed him the day before. These seemingly tough guys eagerly lined up so Albert could pray for them. Then my dad led them in a powerful prayer, which they prayed fervently, "Lord deliver me from my past, from the nightmares that haunt me, I give myself to You and only You."

Ramon Isaza, one of their main leaders, was healed of multiple diseases. These men had seen the movie at a premiere Lisa and a few others had done weeks before. Lisa says this was one of the most powerful presentations to which she had ever been. By the end of the film, the men were so moved they clapped for about three minutes. Jorge Pirata and Julian, two of the main characters of the true events of *La Montaña*, had been there. They had sent a video message to my dad inviting him to go and visit them.

Unfortunately, when we went with Albert, Jorge Pirata was in court. Julian had been sent to another prison in Medellin and just happened to be in La Picota prison when the movie was presented. Lisa was profoundly moved by the response. Up until that point, guerrillas, soldiers, and country farmers had all loved the movie, but we were curious to see how the paramilitary would respond. When I arrived at the prison with my dad and Albert, the paramilitary men did not hesitate to go and be prayed for.

# CHAPTER 33

# Jorge the Pirate

Jorge Pirata had been one of the supreme paramilitary leaders in the eastern plains of Colombia until the day he surrendered to the government to pay his penance in a jail in Bogotá. As a commander, he had operated from the same town in which my parents were raised and had much respect in his heart for my dad. He gave his men orders not to hurt us but to help us any way they could.

When I was in a paramilitary controlled town filming a documentary, two armed men on motorcycles stopped me and said I could not film without their permission. I lowered my camera and thanked them for warning me. Then they asked me who I was and I said, "I'm Alethia, Martin's daughter."

They immediately became kind and said, "Oh, we are so sorry. Go ahead and film whatever you want." Their change in behavior was the result of my dad's years of friendship with Jorge Pirata and Cuchillo, another paramilitary leader and main character in *La Montaña*.

In December 2013, after Jorge Pirate had served eight years in prison, my dad and I were finally able to visit him. Our friend, Carlos, set the whole thing up and got us in. Deanne Alford, the American lady reporter who came to Colombia to interview all the different sides of the conflict accompanied us. We walked through several security posts and came to his prison ward, the same one we had been to the time before.

Jorge Pirata and his right-hand ideologist named Jaime were waiting for us. Despite their behavior as commanders, they always showed kindness toward us. I last saw them in Casivare, a remote village in the middle of the eastern plains of Colombia. My whole family and I had driven through tough, dry, unpaved roads for hours, and the town was full of paramilitary warriors, armed to the teeth and looking very intimidating. Jorge Pirata had taken one of the bars that had an outdoor deck and ordered the owners to give it to my dad for the day so the whole town could gather around and hear the preaching.

They set up the loudspeakers, and my dad, Canadian evangelist Len Carter, and Javier Vargas (a Colombian lawyer and a good friend of ours who hosts the radio program called *The Truth about the Truth*) began to preach. The paramilitary men rounded up the people and provided a security ring around the meeting area.

Len Carter spoke with passion, "The heart of man is evil." He preached with conviction. "But God came to change our hearts."

Then Javier Vargas took the stage and spoke with as much fervor as he does for the radio stations. "It is not about disarming our hands." He spoke with vehemence. "What we need to do is disarm our hearts, because when a soldier, a guerrilla or a paramilitary is armed, not only are his hands armed, his heart is armed too!"

After the meeting, the paramilitaries and the town people gathered by the hundreds to receive literature and Bibles. Little did we know how much visits like this one would impact Jorge Pirata.

When we got to the prison, a former paramilitary came up to my dad with a huge smile and said, "Martin, you gave me your book *Rescue the Captors* years ago, and I have kept it all this time because I wanted you to sign it for me." My dad gladly signed the book.

This event in Casivare had taken place more than ten years before our visit, and I was wondering what it would be like to see Don Jorge again and what kind of person he had become. When we arrived, he gave us the most affectionate hugs, and I could tell he was just as happy to see us as we were to see him. We sat down, and he served us some soda pop from his fridge. A loud Norteña music group was playing, so he had us crowd into his prison cell, which was a homey, little room with just enough space for a bed and couch. I sat on the bed next to him, and my dad, Carlos Garzón, and Deanne Alford sat on the small couch.

Deanne began by asking him what he thought of the peace negotiations in Cuba, and Don Jorge said it was premature to say anything. My dad agreed and said the only thing that produced any lasting results was when God began to change each and every heart. Jorge Pirata added, "The only one who is going to help us overcome all these problems and difficulties is God, and if He is not placed first, nothing will come of it."

That reminded me of when I spoke to Pablo Catatumbo with Luis Humberto. Ten years before, when the events of *La Montaña* were taking place, my dad and Noel had written a seven-point peace plan. While rummaging through old boxes in our house, we found it and sent it to Noel so he could give it to the FARC delegation. During the meeting, I told them that one of the seven points was for the guerrillas to talk directly to the army generals in an effort to end the war. One reason my dad and Noel suggested this was they knew talking to an intellectual who gets facts from books is different from when the two sides talking actually know what it is like to lose men, to fight, to hike, to live endless days in rain and sweat in the jungle.

As soon as I told Pablo and Ivan the point about talking to

the generals, Santrich spoke up and said, "But Alethia, remember, that is not the first point."

I turned to him in surprise, "Oh, I know it's not the first point; it's just one of the points. I don't really remember the order."

Santrich corrected me and said, "The first point is that all sides must place God first." Now Jorge Pirata was reminding me again of that most important point.

I asked Jaime, the paramilitary ideologist, what he thought of the possibility that the FARC leaders in Havana might not serve a prison term. He said, "We don't really care if they go to prison or not, as long as the FARC organization ceases to exist. A prison term is the least of our concerns. What truly matters is that they also change their ways, as we have done."

His comment was right on. What good is a prison full of people running their illegal operations from within? The only thing changed is the location of the problem. The illegal action could take place in the jungles of Colombia, on the beaches of Cuba, or from within a prison cell in Bogotá. The answer is simple: the heart needs to change. Then it won't matter where they are.

When Lisa and I wrote the script, we wanted every detail to be as true as possible so the real characters portrayed in it would like it. It was remarkable for me to hear Don Jorge speak of the movie. He told us what happened after the guerrillas confused one of their paramilitary commanders with a priest. It eventually resulted in a peace accord on one of the most fought-over mountains in the region.

Don Jorge recounted the story. "We had come to the agreement that we wouldn't attack the civilians under their control, and they wouldn't attack the civilians under our control. So there were many important steps that we were developing. When somebody asks me about the movie, I just respond, 'That was all real.' And thanks to God nothing bad happened, and we started getting closer to our enemies.

"I'm going to be honest with you Martin. I thank God for your family's visits to me. They helped me so much personally that it led to my demobilization and my men surrendering as well. And I thank you and your wife for everything you told me and all you invested in me. I say this with all the sincerity in the world, fully convinced that I will never return to the war. Never."

Then he told of how the other guerrilla fronts shown in *La Montaña* had also wanted to surrender when they saw the paramilitaries doing it. The guerrilla commanders talked to Jorge Pirata about that possibility, but the High Commissioner for Peace during that period told the paramilitaries they had to give up their weapons or they would be killed.

As a result, Don Jorge told the guerrillas to wait because it was getting complicated. He said, "We can't guarantee that it will go well for you guys because we don't know how it will go for us." This caused the guerrillas to desist from surrendering, but with a little encouragement from my dad and my uncle Chaddy, Jorge Pirata laid down his arms with Cuchillo and his men. They surrendered on April 11, 2006.

Unfortunately, Cuchillo later changed his mind and continued as a paramilitary commander and died a tragic death. My grandparents on my dad's side of the family, especially my grandpa who had a big heart for him, were extremely sad when they heard the news. Ever since Cuchillo was a little boy, he was one of the many kids that my grandparents helped by paying a basic school fee and making sure he had the adequate school shoes and supplies he needed. My dad would give his family, who were really poor, fish from his fishing business. There were bonds that had taken years to form.

Noel had sent a gift for Jorge – a signed copy of *La Montaña*.

In it he wrote, "This message is my commitment with all my friends from work to the greatest desire that the Colombian family has, which is peace with social justice. – Noel."

Jorge Pirata smiled as he read the note and asked me to give Noel his gratitude. Carlos, who worked directly with Sergio Jaramillo, one of the government's top peace negotiators, wanted proof of the truthfulness of the film and asked Don Jorge what his relationship had been like with Noel, his enemy. Don Jorge replied, "We treated each other with respect, as true gentlemen do." (A few days after our visit to the prison, I got a call from Carlos saying that Sergio Jaramillo wanted to see the movie. I gave Carlos three copies for him.)

For the next hour, Jorge Pirata told us about Restitution of Victims, a government program that had given him much peace of mind. He told story after story of the families who had forgiven him. He said, "Out of forty-nine families, forty-seven have forgiven me. Before, I couldn't sleep at night. I would toss and turn thinking about all the damage I had caused. But now that I am facing our victims, I feel peace and I can rest at night. It is the most difficult moment, the hardest thing to do, but it is the most beautiful thing in life. After doing two acts of reconciliation a day, I would get to my bed and sleep as I had never slept before. I read the Holy Bible every single day." They wrote a book about it called *The Reconciliation,* which can be found on www.fiscalia.com.

Then my dad said to Jorge, "You know, the men who are in Cuba negotiating with the government reached the point where they accepted that one day they are going to ask the country for forgiveness in general terms. But, I think it is necessary to be specific and share these kinds of stories, because it is necessary that they go through something similar to truly obtain peace. Although standing in front of the country and admitting there were victims and asking them for forgiveness is a good start, it will be never be complete without facing specific cases."

Jorge agreed and said, "Yes, it's the only way that you can have peace."

My dad added, "And not only for you but for the victims, because when they open their hearts to forgive, you get healed and they also get healed."

I had met people whom God was beginning to change – people on all sides of the war – but I had never seen anyone with as contrite heart and humble spirit as Jorge Pirata. King David in the Bible says one of the things God will not reject is a contrite heart and a humble spirit. I felt the pain in his bones as he told every story of when he had to face his victims. His eyes watered up when he told us about all the times the people had genuinely forgiven him.

By the end of his talk, I felt so much love for him that I said, "Don Jorge, I feel in my heart I need to tell you something." He closed the door of his cell; I guess so he could hear me better and dedicate his full attention to what I was going to say. As I was trying hard to fight back tears, I said, "Don Jorge, God has forgiven you. And not only that, but He has also forgotten. He doesn't remember any of the things you did anymore, so you shouldn't remember them either."

# CHAPTER 34

# General Barrero

For years my dad had worked alongside General Barrero in the western part of the country. The general had his own motto: Bad people had a choice between getting *cacao* (a chocolate farm) or *plomo* (which means lead) from the army. If the bad people changed their attitude, the army would try to help them leave the war and start planting crops. If they insisted on continuing with acts of terrorism, then they would get war. My dad was always called on to increase the radio coverage in the areas where it was most needed. This produced visible results, and even though the general did not claim to be a protestant Christian, he could not deny the results the peace campaign had on the area he commanded. Soon, many other generals and colonels started getting a hint of what was happening, and the army became one of our greatest allies for what God was doing in the country.

To demonstrate what God was beginning to do with the army, I will share what Ever wrote from the emerald mines of Musso. (My dad wrote Ever's story in Part I.)

One day a lady I had evangelized said, "Brother, I've listened to the radio and its messages are wonderful. Could you give me a radio for my son who is a professional soldier and is on a high mountain military base where there are many guerrillas?"

So of course, I gave her two Galcom radios, and one of them was sent to her son.

The sergeant who was in charge of the squad approached her son, the soldier, and three other friends. When he saw the radio, the sergeant asked, "Where did you get that radio?"

The soldier responded, "A missionary friend of my mom's gave it to her."

The sergeant said, "I know those radios because I used to have one in Meta where I worked before. Its messages were wonderful and I gave mine to my mother. I'll pay you 100,000 pesos (the equivalent of fifty dollars) for that radio."

The soldier replied, "I can't, because my mother told me to listen to the messages of this radio; she said it would be my protection."

So the sergeant said, "I'll give you an order soldier. At 12:00 p.m. and at 6:00 p.m., you will turn on the radio, and all the soldiers who are available will sit and listen to the messages. This is an order!" And that is how the Lord penetrated the mountains of the northeastern part of Colombia. The soldier's mother later told me that more than 70 percent of the men in that military base walked with the Lord.

Whenever General Barrero got transferred to a new area, the first thing he would do was call my dad, and they would make plans to set up strategic radio stations in the most violent areas. It is ironic that when Noel was in charge of a mountain or an area, he would do the exact same thing. If a group of Indians was causing trouble with riots and madness, the general would have us set up premieres of *La Montaña*, and thousands of Indians would attend. For years, the areas in which General Barrero and Noel worked in were pacified.

Just as it was a good surprise for us to discover that Noel was a member of the FARC delegation in Havana, it was a great day when President Santos named General Barrero the

Commanding General of the entire Armed Forces of Colombia. Now the work he and my dad had been doing in the western part of the country could take place in every corner.

One of the first things General Barrero did in his new position was hold a special event to honor my dad in front of hundreds of the high-ranking officers that were being promoted. I tagged along because I wanted to see what it was like to watch the Commanding General of the Armed Forces of Colombia give a speech. I got up early to meet with my dad and Luis Humberto. We arrived at a military officers' club in Bogotá and entered a huge auditorium full of about five hundred officers, from majors to colonels, all dressed in their best uniforms and ready to receive their commander.

Before General Barrero entered, an announcement was made to inform everyone to please excuse his combat gear. He had just returned by helicopter after being in the jungle with his men. This was typical of Barrero. He wanted to be where the action was and dreaded the thought of being locked into a four-walled office in Bogotá. Out he came with his camouflage uniform and combat boots on. As soon as he walked in, everyone stood up and saluted him with utmost respect, and he began his almost two-hour-long speech.

If a book was ever written about Colombia's best speeches, this one should be in it. He made you want to do everything better and serve your country as best you could. Few speeches, especially given by generals, are that inspiring. But more than that, he seemed a hundred percent genuine and honest. He spoke from his heart and motivated his soldiers to continue with the difficult task at hand. "We have the greatest opportunity now to give our best for our country. We need to take it, or else it will pass us by, and we will wonder if we could have given more of ourselves. This is a war of details. You can't let anything escape. Anything you despise, even the simplest thing, will be the cause of your defeat.

"People think I am crazy because I care about the soldiers' socks. But they are important. The socks used to slip off their feet and stick to the bottom of their boots, but I made sure to change that because the soldiers' comfort matters. Many details are important. We can't say to a *campesino* (a farmer) who asks us for help when someone is stealing his cattle that it is not our problem. Yes, it is our problem, and we need to find ways to help them, or else Don Ivan Márquez will come and do it for us!"

Then he came to the most important part, the reason he had announced this occasion in the first place. On a screen he showed a map full of red dots where all the different radio stations were.

"I want you all to meet Martin. Please stand up, Martin. Martin is the one who has been supporting us with all these radio stations. Seven radio stations have been strategically placed in the central and western mountain range. Martin has helped us fix our own radio stations. One of our stations was off the air for three years, and I asked for help. Martin came and fixed it for us. What is the purpose of these radio stations? It is so those who are good can continue being good. And, so those who are bad can change as a result of the messages they hear.

"You cannot go to Puerto Tejado to plant coffee and cacao because they don't have that culture. Instead, you have to show up with Salsa and music schools. If you go to Armenia, you have to speak to them about tourism. These radio stations that Martin has constructed have allowed this to happen. They are very important. So in those areas we distribute these radios that Martin gives us."

He took out a little green Galcom radio from his pocket and showed it to everyone.

"These radios have a solar panel and rechargeable batteries.

They broadcast one or two of the radio stations. Soldiers have them, the rural communities receive them, and the guerrillas also carry them. Martin also gives out these parachutes."

He took out the familiar small parachutes that many of our friends in the United States and Canada had been faithfully sewing for years. My dad has been tying books, Bibles, and radios to these parachutes and throwing them into the jungle from his airplane for years.

The general continued explaining, "These parachutes carry religious books and New Testaments so people can have a different attitude. This does not harm anyone, and it has helped us to gain control of an area that was lost. Or how was Cauca doing in June of last year? People have been voluntarily eradicating the illicit harvest of the cocaine fields."

General Barrero showed a picture of Santander de Quilichao in which the Indians were eradicating the illegal mines. Then he showed an article written in 2011 in which he said Cauca would be different in three years as a result of this hard work. "Today Cauca is different," he stated.

On the screen a picture of a five-year-old girl carrying a machine gun appeared side by side with another picture in which she was back with her family.

"The children from the past and the children now with their coffee plantations. Look at Marcelino in this picture and look at Marcelino in the next picture.

"On the big projector were two pictures, one of an Indian with a mob beating a policeman and in the next photo he was completely different as he took care of a coffee farm with more than three million plants.

"Today the Indian communities have been timidly approaching us, and the commander of each battalion talks with them to make sure they have the necessary truck for their work. The private sector lends us the fertilizer needed for their crops because either they are going to get lead (war) or cacao from us. So they decide what they want. We can give them either one depending on their attitude. The end of war is not accomplished only with your heads but also with your hearts, and I thank all the special guests. Thank you so much for your presence with us."

He signaled my dad to stand up and said, "So when you see Martin installing radio stations up in the mountains, please don't take him out!" Everyone applauded fervently and the meeting ended.

My dad and I went back to Havana shortly after that in December of 2013 with Deanne Alford, the American journalist. In Cuba, Deanne confessed to me that she was really nervous about interviewing these guys. She said, "I feel as though this is the moment I've been preparing for my whole life. I wasn't even this nervous when I interviewed President Bush. I think this is very important."

The next day Ivan, Santrich, Noel, Yuri, my dad, Deanne, and I went to the nice restaurant we had gone to with Clayt Sonmore. We all sat down and ordered drinks, and the interview began. Unlike most of the other people who have interviewed these guys, Deanne asked questions that had never been asked in an official interview before.

She asked them what they thought the role my dad had in encouraging this peace process.

Ivan said, "Martin is an apostle of peace, a man who encourages us on our journey for the search of a political solution to the Colombian conflict. It's something urgent and necessary to put an end to the conflict that's been going on more than fifty years. I want Santrich to add to my words of appreciation."

Santrich confirmed his words and said, "I would say this of him: Martin seems to me to be a magnificent man of truth."

"He's a man of peace," Ivan said as he puffed out some smoke from his cigar.

With sincerity in his tone, Santrich continued, "For some reason, destiny has placed him to always move through the heavens. That is why he moves in the skies in an airplane. Of course, he also goes accompanied by many angels. Then there is Alethia and a number of people who help him a great deal, and not only do they help him, but they also give strength and tremendous energy to approach us. Look, you can certainly say that Martin has filled us with a great deal of optimism and hope to continue forward in this difficult process. Alethia is Martin's angel."

Deanne later asked Ivan if there were any Christians in the FARC, and Ivan turned to Noel and said, "Of course there are! There is San Noel, San Yuri and Santrich."

I turned to Ivan and said, "And what about San Ivan?"

He shook his head sadly and said, "Not yet."

On our last night in Havana, Noel got excited. He always does when he is talking about the Friendship Plan with my dad. "Martin, we can't waste any more time! We have to take advantage of this situation and make as many friends as we possibly can. We don't want these opportunities to run out and for us to have to say, 'Oh, we could have done so much more on that island but we didn't.' That would be unforgivable. What if we arrange a meeting with General Barrero and Timochenko? Or General Barrero and Ivan! That would be brilliant."

My dad nodded in deep thought, "Yes General Barrero could fly in by night. He wouldn't even have to stay a day. He could just stay long enough to have a meeting. The press wouldn't even have to know about it. I wonder if the president would approve that. It would be a huge step in the right direction toward solving this."

Noel affirmed, "Yes, because there is trust. He is your friend and you trust him. That means he is our friend."

Noel was truly the heart and soul behind these encounters.

He had been the one to contact my dad the first time and the one to contact us ever since then, always thinking of whom my dad knew that could help them with their peace initiative.

My dad set up a meeting with General Barrero as soon as we got back to Bogotá. We needed to tell him all the details of our latest trip and discuss the possibility that Noel had recently planted. I had gone to visit the general several times before when he was commanding in Cali and Popayan, but this time was different. A colonel met us outside and I felt as if I was following the main character in an action-packed film going through all the security checkpoints into the inner sanctum of the main vault. We went through locked doors with secret passwords and long, white hallways adorned with swords from the 1800s until we finally got to the last check and made it into a nice living room where they offered us beverages.

My dad ordered tea and I had water. The tea was not any normal tea. It had fruit in it and looked more like a cocktail. The colonel was nice enough to let me re-order my drink as we waited. Soon the general called us into his office, and the guards at the door collected our cell phones.

Barrero greeted us with his characteristic big warm bear hugs, and we walked into his new office – the most beautiful wooden room with a huge desk and a picture of Simon Bolivar behind it. Flags decorated the windows, and we sat in a comfortable living room. Deanne interviewed him in order to get the military's perspective on the war, and as soon as she was done, my dad told her to turn off her recording device so we could continue in privacy.

My dad told the general of our recent trip to Cuba and how the attitude of the men had been changing. He said there was a possibility of Ivan or Timochenko wanting to talk directly to him, but if he felt uncomfortable with that idea, he could send the colonel in his stead for now. This seemed to be the last thing

Barrero was expecting to hear from us. He thought about it for a while and asked why in the world they would want to meet with him. It was all Deanne could do not to laugh because here my dad was coming with what he thought was a completely normal idea, and the general obviously thought otherwise. In an effort to help get my dad's point across, I explained to him the situation I had seen.

"The thing is, mi General, the guerrillas over there are talking to people they don't trust. There is no trust between them and the government's delegation. The person they trust is my dad. And the only reason they trust him is because he has been forming a friendship with them ever since his kidnapping thirty years ago. And the only reason they are willing to trust you is because you are my dad's friend and my dad can vouch for you that you are an honest and upright general."

My dad added, "They think that if they surrender to the people they are talking with now, those people will not be true to their word. The reason they want to talk to you is because now there is finally someone in power who is capable of guaranteeing that if they surrender, it won't backfire on them."

I continued pleading with him, "Mi General, if you meet with them, they might even take you out to meet Timochenko. So far, we have talked to Pablo, Ivan, Santrich, and Granda, and the Lord has touched them all, but we need to get to the main leader. This would be a great opportunity to do that."

He thought about it for a while and replied, "I understand what you're saying, Alethia. But I need you to understand that I have to be prudent. I can't just tell the president and Sergio Jaramillo that I want to barge in on their peace plan because somehow I think I know how to do it better. That would hurt their pride and make it seem like the army is trying to take over the process. I need to be wise and wait until they need my help, and they call me."

I said, "You are absolutely right, mi General. We must be prudent, and it is better to be asked for help than to help and have it turn badly on you. I guess we must wait."

"Yes, we have to wait and the right time will come."

# CHAPTER 35

# The National Anthem

A few months after we met with General Barrero, the 2014 Soccer World Cup began. As in any Latin country, soccer is a huge part of our culture. The word to describe what people feel when our country strikes a goal is pure passion and indescribable patriotism. It had been sixteen years since we last contested in a World Cup, and the country was ecstatic. As I watched the first game against Greece with my family in Bogotá, I could picture Jorge Pirata watching it with his paramilitary guys in jail and shouting as we struck our first goal. I could see Ivan Márquez and Santrich watching it in Cuba and wondered if they were celebrating the goals with my dad, Luis Humberto, and Albert who were visiting them. I imagined the president, congressmen and senators all proud of their country and the soldiers and guerrillas finding creative ways to watch it in the jungle or at least hear it live from their little radios. I could see the farmers in the countryside, crying for joy, and Noel's face of contentment.

Before the game started, the Colombian national anthem began, and I had to fight back tears when I saw the look of James Rodriguez's face as he sang passionately. He is one of Colombia's most beloved players, and this was the moment he had been waiting for his whole life. He was absorbing his dream that had come true – representing Colombia in a World Cup. The entire country sang with him:

> *Oh, unfading glory!*
> *Oh, immortal jubilee!*
> *In furrows of pain,*
> *The good now germinates.*

We had barely finished singing the first part of the anthem when it was cut short and the music stopped. The reporters announced that the Greek anthem would now begin. The tens of thousands of Colombians in the stadium thought otherwise and completely overpowered the Greek anthem by singing the rest of the anthem with no music to cover their bare voices:

> *The fearful night has ceased.*
> *Sublime Liberty shines forth*
> *the dawning of its invincible light.*
> *All of mankind, groaning in chains,*
> *understands the words*
> *of the one who died on the cross.*

With our hands to our hearts, the whole country sang with them the last verse a cappella. The game started and before we knew it, we had made our first goal. We won 3 to 0 that day, and after every goal, the first thing the players would do was lift their heads to the sky and point as if toward God in gratitude to Him. My dad said in one of his sermons now transcribed in *The Book of Daniel*, the Lord turned King Nebuchadnezzar's seven years of insanity the moment he lifted his head toward the skies to the only One who can give a sound mind.

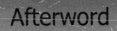

# Afterword

*By Russell Stendal*

On June 11, 2014, I found myself once again on an airplane headed for Havana with Albert, Luis Humberto, and David Cutsforth. We landed at 1:00 a.m., and a lady from Cuban Immigration began to quiz me on what she thought the purpose of our journey. "What church are you affiliated with?" she asked with a frown. "Have you come to preach in Cuba?" She relentlessly continued to probe for any hidden agenda.

I discreetly insisted, to no avail, that we had only come to visit friends and spend a few days by the sea. Finally, I replied, "We are friends of the delegation of the FARC, and they are expecting us." After that we got royal treatment.

Noel and Ernesto were outside and drove us to a nice cottage by the side of the ocean. For five days we had a wonderful time, as the guerrillas would show up early in the morning for prayer. Several notable miracles took place as Albert prayed for the sick. David shared songs he had written that were based on his favorite Scripture passages, and I translated.

## Galatians 5

> 22 *But the fruit of the Spirit is this: Charity, joy, peace, tolerance, gentleness, goodness, faith,*
>
> 23 *meekness, temperance: against such there is no law.*

On Saturday June 14, we found ourselves sitting in the bedroom of Ivan Márquez, inside the special compound called El Laguito in a large mansion that had reportedly been built by the former dictator in the 1950s, watching a World Cup soccer game. The entire house was decked out with special photographs that had been gathered for the celebration on May 27 of the fiftieth anniversary of the FARC. Now, here we were watching Colombia play Greece with an inner circle of Colombian revolutionaries who were very proud of their country.

Colombia won 3-0. This was one of the most extraordinary experiences of my life. A Cuban colonel in charge of security stuck his head into the room and was surprised to find the inner sanctum full of Americans! He smiled brightly and shook all of our hands. Rodrigo Granda and Pablo Catatumbo also came in and greeted us.

I had previously informed Albert that I knew that Pablo had an old wound that still bothered him on his right arm and shoulder. We were not sure how to broach the subject of praying for his infirmity so I told Albert to be ready. When Pablo greeted him, Albert grabbed his right hand, put his left arm around Pablo's shoulder, and with no further protocol immediately began to pray. There were lots of scars and stitches and a big metal plate still imbedded in his right shoulder. I got my arm around his left shoulder and also began to pray. There was a look of amazement on Pablo's face as God began to touch the tough, old warrior.

After a few seconds, I explained that Albert was also an old soldier who had been injured on numerous occasions during his twenty-four years of military service. I also introduced David and explained that he was a businessman who had been a great help to our ministry in Colombia over the years. We had a wonderful talk with Pablo. He even authorized Albert to continue to pray for him as much as he wanted.

A few minutes later we went into a back room where Yuri,

the FARC dentist, fixed a broken tooth for Luis Humberto, a cousin to Colombian President Santos. Then we made plans to get together with Noel on Sunday, June 15, to watch the Colombian presidential election returns.

Our guide and driver, Ernesto, picked the Hemingway Marina for the occasion. This is a very beautiful spot, and we spent a memorable Sunday evening watching the win of President Santos, which ensures the peace process will continue during his second term.

On Monday June 16, as we were leaving for the airport, the guerrilla leaders took us to the beautiful mansion at El Laguito one more time so they could say goodbye. Rodrigo Granda, known as the chancellor of the FARC, had stopped by our house in the morning, and we were able to have a nice session with him in which it was very clear that we have his love and respect.

Then, Ivan Márquez and Jesus Santrich had a special meeting with us. Ivan thanked us from the bottom of his heart and told us that we have played a very important role in the peace process. He said – his eyes clear and sparkling – that we had helped him to see and understand the importance of forgiving his enemies and asking for forgiveness from the many victims of the war. Ivan asked me to translate this to Albert Luepnitz and David Cutsforth as he told them how much he appreciates both of them. He was also very grateful for Clayt Sonmore.

As we were leaving, Luis Humberto pinned a special emblem of a dove (the emblem of President Santos) on the chest of Ivan Márquez as he tactfully reminded the guerrillas that almost half of the country did not vote for President Santos and, therefore, do not support his peace initiative. It will continue to be a long, slow, process, as each individual must deal with his or her own heart. It is now up to the guerrillas to win the trust of the country. It is up to the president and the government to recognize that only God can change human hearts and invite the Prince of Peace to have his rightful place in Colombia.

# Sin vs. Liberty

*By Russell Stendal*

## Psalm 32

Of David, Maschil

*1 Blessed is he whose transgression is forgiven, whose sin is covered.*

*2 Blessed is the man unto whom the LORD does not impute iniquity and in whose spirit there is no guile.*

*Maschil* means "for understanding."

Thirty-two is eight times four. Eight is the number of new beginnings in Christ, and four is the number that represents the heavenly love of God. His love is not like human love. His love is not primarily an emotion. It incorporates a decision. The heavenly Father gave his only begotten Son. The Son chose to do the will of the Father and give his life so we might be redeemed. The love of God springs from sacrifice and redeems by its very nature. We are to have a new beginning so God's love may flow in and through us.

Sin is one thing, iniquity is another thing, and rebellion is yet something else.

Sin is to simply go against the Word of the Lord, but iniquity is to do it knowingly and cover it up. This is serious.

Some theologians teach a doctrine of *imputed righteousness.* (Clever men have figured out a way for God to pretend they are fine, when in reality they are still contaminated with iniquity.) Here we have the possibility of *imputed iniquity.* This is when fools think they are fine, and God says that they are still hiding something ugly.

*Guile* has to do with a hidden agenda. The hidden agenda has to do with men trying to use God to get what they want, instead of being willing to do what God wants no matter what the cost.

The cost will always include the death of the old man, the old nature. This is why Jesus says to deny yourself, pick up your cross, and follow him if you wish to be his disciple (Matthew 16:24; Mark 8:34). A cross does not provide instant death for the old nature. It is not a bullet in the head to the desires and temptations of the flesh. It is a long and slow death. It is anguish as the life of flesh slowly bleeds to death drop by drop. Scripture encourages us to take up our cross daily.

The Lord can decide to forgive or not forgive it, and in the Bible there are cases when the Lord did not forgive someone.

Rebellion is even worse than iniquity, for the rebellious take up arms against the Lord or against someone that he has sent. Rebellion is to join the enemy. The one who is in rebellion does not even attempt to hide it. They wear it on their sleeve.

> 3 *When I kept silence, my bones waxed old through my roaring all the day long.*

> 4 *For day and night thy hand was heavy upon me: my green growth is turned into the drought of summer. Selah.*

*Selah* means "to stop and think about it."

At one time, David attempted to hide his sin, but then a moment came when he had an opportunity to be honest about it. The Lord sent him a prophet who confronted him. After the confrontation, he chose to admit that he was the one who had sinned.

> 5 *I acknowledged my sin unto thee, and I have not hid my iniquity. I said, I will confess (against myself) my rebellions unto the LORD, and thou shalt forgive the iniquity of my sin. Selah.*

> 6 *For this shall every one that is merciful pray unto thee in the time when thou may be found...*

This says that there is a time when the Lord may be found, and our situation may still be resolved with the Lord, but there is a time when this is no longer possible. Jesus said, "Blessed are the merciful, for they shall obtain mercy."

By the time King Saul went to the witch of Endor, there was nothing more that could be done. Scripture relates that God did not forgive him. Prior to his out-and-out rebellion with the witch, Saul had thrown his spear at David and moved on to the point where he killed all the priests. The episode with the witch was just prior to his grand finale when he fell on his own sword and died. The Philistines killed his son Jonathan, beloved by David, because Jonathan had not been able to break the strong soul tie with his father.

> 6 *... surely in the floods of great waters they shall not come near unto him.*

There are merciful ones, and there are floods of great waters. David was chosen by God to be king over Israel when, at the age of about twelve, he showed a merciful heart for his sheep. He was willing to risk his life and kill any lion or bear that went after his flock. God saw that and decided to have Samuel anoint

David king over Israel. However, it took eighteen long hard years of severe anguish and persecution before God thought David was ready to rule over Judah at age thirty.

> 6 For this shall every one that is merciful pray unto thee in the time when thou may be found; surely in the floods of great waters they shall not come near unto him.

We all have situations when we know that we have failed in one way or another. The more serious the sin, the more the Devil is able to work against us.

Everyone who has sinned will feel these floods of great waters. They will enter into a depression where they will think that God has not forgiven them. If God has forgiven them, then they are still unable to do anything useful for God because the enemy keeps stirring up guilt, reminding them of the problem. Or, this could crystallize in the opposite direction as the person affirms his rebellion and openly opposes God.

> 7 Thou art my hiding place; thou shalt preserve me from trouble; thou shalt compass me about with songs of deliverance. Selah.

Where the Spirit of the Lord is, there is liberty – liberty to do the will of God.

This is what the Devil does not want us to understand, for the Lord can even forgive rebellion and free us. When he places us in liberty, he does not remember our past. If he does not remember our past, then we should not allow the Devil to mention it. The sacrifice system of the Old Testament spent just as much emphasis dealing with guilt as it did dealing with sin. Both must be brought to light, bled to death at the altar of God, and then burned into a pile of ashes on the altar when the fire of God is applied to the entire mess (Leviticus 7).

In the New Testament, all the promises are yea and amen

in Christ. He was the supreme sacrifice (Romans 5:10). We are reconciled to God by his death, but we shall be saved by his life. Our salvation is in him. He is the gift of God. The Father gave his only Son. We must be willing to bring our sin, our iniquity, our rebellion, and our guilt and hand them over for him. As our new High Priest of the order of Melchisedec and as the only Mediator of the new covenant, he will supervise the altar and make sure that our sin and guilt are bled to death and the fire of the Holy Spirit of God cleanses us.

In the new covenant, the gospel is very similar to the altar in the old covenant. The true gospel represents the conditions under which God will receive us. *For if we confess our sin, he is faithful and just not only to forgive us, but also to cleanse us from all unrighteousness* (1 John 1:9; Titus 2:14). When he cleanses us from all unrighteousness, it might not seem all that comfortable at the time – when he applies the sword of the Spirit and separates the soul and spirit, when he circumcises our hearts, when he runs us through the fire of his dealings to make sure that we are refined and purified as fine gold. Yet he promises that if we are willing to suffer with him, we will also reign with him (Romans 8:17-18).

When he places us into liberty, it is conditioned on various things. The most important is that we are to forgive others. For if we do not forgive others, it is possible to lose the liberty that we have. If we do not forgive, we will not be forgiven (Mark 11:25-26).

The only way to truly forgive is by the grace of God, for when the Lord forgives, he forgets. As humans we are incapable of this.

Many think they have forgiven, but the situation continues to eat away at them. This might go on and on. If it continues, they will go from bad to worse. If they refuse to forgive, they will be eaten away by sin, even if they had been an innocent victim.

Whatever happened will continue to hammer away at them.

It will continue to pierce them and it will never leave. In the end, even if they were a victim, it will become an obsession. They will not be able to think of anything else. They will not be able to let go of it. If it becomes an obsession and they are unable to let it go, it will become like a prison. While they are in bondage, it will be impossible for them to enjoy the liberty of the Spirit of God.

> 7 *Thou art my hiding place; thou shalt preserve me*
> *from trouble; thou shalt compass me about with*
> *songs of deliverance. Selah.*

Where did the trouble (this word could also have been translated *anguish*) come from?

The anguish comes when there is hidden sin. The anguish comes when we have been mistreated and have not released it to the Lord. The anguish continues when we refuse to repay evil with good.

The only way to stop the anguish is for us to be hidden in the life of Christ. If we are hidden in the life of Christ, no one and no thing will be able to touch us. No one and no thing will be able to take away our peace no matter what the external circumstances.

However, even if the Lord has forgiven us of something grave and serious or if we have forgiven someone else of something grave and serious (there are many people who have multiple issues of both categories), scarring will always occur. These scars may not be visible, for they are scars in the soul.

For example, I may look fine, but I have a lot of scars on my body. Some of them are the result of things that I did that were not prudent, accidents in my youth, etc.

In addition to those injuries, I also have scars on my body that came from my enemies. Some of the most serious scars actually came from those who I thought at the time were my friends.

When I am having a good day and everything is going perfectly and I stretch my muscles before doing any serious exercise, I can get through the day in a more or less normal fashion. But I have other days that are not so normal. There are nights, and places in particular, when I do not sleep well. I have fractured bones and damaged vertebrae, along with pulled tendons and a lot of muscle damage. Some of this came from being tied to a tree and tortured for five months at the hands of my enemies. Some of it has come as a result of thirty years of dangerous missionary expeditions back into enemy territory to rescue the captors.

I have days when everything hurts, and I have been unable to rest for many nights. It is easy to become cross and agitated. And I am still referring only to physical scars, not to the scars in the soul.

When I write for extended periods of time and concentrate at my computer, it causes my muscles to become tense. Afterwards it is easy to tear something loose. Each time the old scars are torn open, they are harder to heal.

Now, if we examine the soul through the Lord's eyes, we realize that our soul can have similar problems. We know that we can have scars in the natural realm of our bodies, and the scars do not heal perfectly. We know that it is possible for similar things to happen in the realm of the soul.

In another Psalm David wrote, "He restores my soul" (Psalm 23).

David knew this from first-hand experience. He knew that he had accumulated deep wounds and scars in his soul that only God could erase.

There is another factor that contributes to these situations. Even when the Lord forgives our sin, our iniquity, and our rebellion, the consequences continue to advance until they run their long and tortuous course. This happens even after we are absolved of our guilt.

After he was forgiven, David never forgot the sentence that he had indirectly given himself, for he was in the strange position of being both the guilty party and the king responsible for judging the case. God worked it out so David inadvertently sentenced himself (2 Samuel 12:1-14).

The prophet Nathan came and told David about two people. One had a flock of sheep and many things. He was a very wealthy person. His neighbor was a poor man and only had one little lamb that was the family pet.

Nathan told the king that instead of killing one of his own flock, the rich man decided to party with his friends and killed the poor man's only lamb.

David's shepherd heart was inflamed. "That man deserves to die," he exclaimed!

But David also had some mercy left in his heart, so he said the rich man should repay fourfold.

Then Nathan had to tell King David, "You are that man!"

And as a result of that sin, David lost four sons – each one under extremely painful circumstances.

After he was forgiven, even after he knew that God had blotted out his rebellion and would remember it no more, David continued to see other problems begin to affect his sons. He knew there was continuous danger and that his sentence would be extended because God Himself had declared that the sword would always be upon David and his house. Bathsheba lost her first child right away, and then Absalom killed Amnon. Later Absalom entered into rebellion and briefly took the kingdom away from David and was killed after Joab found him hanging by his hair from a tree.

The fourth son, Adonijah, died after David's death.

Even someone as great as Abraham, who is listed in Scripture as the friend of God and the father of those who have faith, got into a lot of trouble (anguish) when he decided to do things his own way. He considered that his wife was too old to bear him the heir that God had promised. He made up a plan, with the consent of his wife Sarah, to help God out.

Remember the story of how Abraham begat Ishmael with the Egyptian handmaid, Hagar? Then Sarah gave birth to Isaac, the promised heir, when she was ninety years old. Sarah had laughed when she overheard God say she would have a child in her old age. God had the last laugh, and the promised son was named Isaac (laughter).

God dealt with Abraham regarding this situation, and apparently Abraham was okay. We know God forgave him. However, the sons of Isaac and the sons of Ishmael are still in conflict with one another four thousand years later.

> 8 *I will instruct thee and teach thee in the way*
> *which thou shalt go; I will fix mine eyes upon thee.*
>
> 9 *Be ye not as the horse or as the mule, which have*
> *no understanding: whose mouth must be held in*
> *subjection with bit and bridle, or they will not come*
> *near unto thee.*
>
> 10 *There are many sorrows for the wicked; but he*
> *that waits in the LORD, mercy shall compass him*
> *round about.*

The Lord "compassing us in mercy" means he will continue to have a place in his heart for us. The word for mercy is related to the word for heart in Hebrew. His dealings with us, even when they are hard, will always be for our good.

There are those who consider themselves to be good Christians. They feel that they are wise in the things of the Lord, and they have great understanding of the Word – and sometimes this is the case.

But the Devil was also wise and had a lot of understanding in the Word, but there was one thing that he did not want to accept, and it began to bother him.

After all the importance that Lucifer had in heaven, after all the spectacular gifts that were given him, and after all the confidence that was entrusted to him – for he is one of only three archangels mentioned in Scripture – he thought that surely he was the right hand of the Lord. And what did God do?

God created a little human creature called Adam, and right after Adam was created, God gave him a lot of responsibility. The Scripture explicitly states that Adam was given dominion over every creature including dominion over every serpent (Genesis 1:28).

There is something else that we must understand, even though it is not so easy to see. The cherubim of God do not have only one face. The cherubim that Ezekiel saw had four faces (Ezekiel 10:14).

It appears that the cherubim can take whatever form they please. Lucifer chose to appear to Eve as a serpent. The cherubim can also take the form of a man. The angels that accompanied the Lord to visit Abraham looked like men. When they visited Sodom and Gomorrah, they looked like men.

But regardless of the face they chose, God had given Adam the dominion, and Lucifer refused to accept this. He sought a way to overturn the divine order and looked for a soft target. He did not try a frontal attack against Adam. He came and deceived Eve.

God had declared that all of the original creation was good, including the serpents. Eve had no reason to believe the serpent was not good. In her experience until that time, all the creatures and all the creation were good. So it was easy to deceive her.

Scripture, however, does not say that Adam was deceived like Eve. It says that Adam rebelled against God.

Eve made a mistake when she listened to the voice of the serpent instead of hearing and obeying Adam and God. What Adam did was much more serious. Adam did not make a simple mistake; he turned his back on God in order to follow Eve. When Adam did this, in effect, he joined the Devil's team. The Devil is eternal, and Adam was mortal. Now Adam is dead, and the Devil has usurped the dominion for close to six thousand years since.

This issue is not yet fully resolved. It is one thing to dictate the sentence, and the Devil has already been sentenced. It is quite another thing to actually apply the sentence.

The Lord Jesus Christ has opened the scroll; he has broken the seals, yet the world is still in the hands of the Devil. In order to apply the sentence, two witnesses are required (Deuteronomy 17:6; 19:15; Revelation 11:3). The trumpets of God are beginning to sound, and soon the Devil and his kingdom will be overthrown by the righteous judgments of God. The Devil rules all the kingdoms of this world, but it is all about to come down (Revelation 11:15).

God made provision for Adam and Eve. When things turned out bad in Eden, he clothed them with coats of skins (Genesis 3:21). In order to get the skins, something had to die. God made them understand immediately that without the shedding of blood, there is no remission (Hebrews 9:22), and none of us can be saved in our own life. Salvation is available only in the life of Christ.

If we are hidden in the life of Christ, it is because our old life had to die. A dead person cannot do anything. The law cannot condemn a dead person because the person is already dead, and the maximum penalty under the law is the death penalty. The wages of sin is death. A dead person cannot even be accused of anything under the law.

> 10 *There are many sorrows for the wicked; but he*
> *that waits in the LORD, mercy shall compass him*
> *round about.*

The only way out for any of us is if the Lord grants us mercy. How does his mercy operate? He does not allow us to continue in our own ways.

The mercy of the Lord is when he enters our sphere and destroys the wonderful concept we have of ourselves. In his mercy, he will destroy every trace of our pride and arrogance.

This is why those who refuse to forgive and who feel so self-righteous tend to cycle between depression and euphoria even after they have been forgiven and healed. Their scars can continue to produce a similar effect each time something or someone revives the old wound. Our hope lies with the fact that Jesus is not only the author of our salvation; he is also in the business of restoring souls (Psalm 23).

We are all more fragile physically than some of us think. I was telling my children that if I could have the opportunity to live my life over again, I would make some changes and do some things differently. I would take better care of my body and not take so many risks. As the years go on, we feel the effects of any scar tissue in our body more and more. Broken bones can heal, but we will always be left with a scar.

So if we can be more prudent when we are young and avoid accidents, our body will be very thankful when we are old. Our soul is the same. If, by the grace of God, we can deal with unforgiveness, bitterness, and resentment, we will have fewer scars in our soul.

> 11 *Be glad in the LORD and rejoice, ye righteous,*
> *and shout for joy, all ye that are upright in heart.*

If the Lord can truly make our heart upright, it is because he has placed his heart in us and his heart reacts differently. He is not willing that any should perish; he does not desire to sink anyone and the heart of God desires to redeem and to lift up. If the heart of God has to effect judgment to stop someone, it is with sadness.

Many think that in ministry they must control everyone – that if we leave the people loose and do not control them, something bad will happen. I have never been a controller, and yes, I have gotten into a bit of trouble over this from time to time, but I do not have the heart to control people. I want to see everyone under the control of the Holy Spirit.

We are not to be as the horse or the mule that must be controlled by a bit and a bridle in someone's heavy hand. For those who are out of control cannot be straightened out by any of us. Only the Lord can straighten them out. So, the more that we leave them in the hands of the Lord, the greater the possibility that the Lord can correct them.

Even so, there are those who do not straighten out, who tend to become very arrogant with their religion. The sublime deception of the enemy is when he is able to convince someone they are righteous because they are complying with religious rites and acts.

This person does not drink, does not smoke, and does not dance; he goes to church and feels quite justified. But what if they don't forgive? (Matthew 6:14-15). This is serious.

This is why in the ministry of the Lord Jesus he said that the publicans and sinners were way ahead of the Pharisees in terms of entering into the kingdom of God. At least the publicans and sinners knew that they were in trouble, but the Pharisees could not see their problem because they felt justified by their own religiosity.

Righteousness cannot be accomplished by any of us on our

own. Only the Lord can accomplish it. But the Lord desires to effect his righteousness in us, for he desires to work in our hearts. When he works in our hearts and cleanses us, then he is able to guide and direct us.

If he is able to cleanse our hearts and if he continues to purify our hearts – and he will not do this against our will – then he will be able to work through us. Do you know what will happen if we refuse to allow him to work in and through us?

If we are not participating in what the Lord is doing, we will never feel truly satisfied. We will never feel that our lives count and that our life is worth living.

Jesus said, "Blessed are those who hunger and thirst for righteousness, for they shall be satisfied" (Matthew 5:6).

Therefore, those who are seeking anything else will never be satisfied.

Satan and his demons will never be satisfied no matter what they obtain because the only way to be truly satisfied is with the life of God. If the life of God is in us, it will flow through us for the benefit of our neighbors and even for the good of our enemies. And the enemies that are the most difficult for us to forgive are those who are the closest to us.

It is much easier to forgive an enemy that is far away, but what about an enemy that lives in our own home or in our same congregation or in our workplace? What about that person over there who has the power and authority we would like to have, and we are confident that we could do their job much better than they can? All day long, every day, we must put up with the mistakes we believe this person makes. If we continue in this line of thinking, the "Lucifer syndrome" can enter.

Why should I submit to the person that God placed in this position? What do they know? I am more qualified. And so Lucifer begins to tighten the screws.

And God in his mercy – for he promises to compass us with

his mercy –does not take us out of the problem. He leaves us there in the midst of the trouble.

Sometimes our trouble (anguish) is very close to us. It may be our spouse. If the trouble is the husband, and the wife somehow manages to get rid of her husband, do you know what will happen? The problem could come back to haunt her in her son. This could be even more difficult to escape. Why would God allow this? Because he wants her to overcome the problem, and the problem cannot be overcome by turning our back and running away from it. We cannot solve the problem by speaking evil of the other party and trying to bring them down.

The problem will only be overcome when we release our desire for revenge and forgive from the heart – when we begin to pray for our enemies and do what the Lord indicates. Evil must be overcome with good.

We must be taught by the Lord, and he must work in and through us because if we attempt to solve our problems on our own, we may end up with an even greater disaster. If we are truly facing someone who is evil, it is not wise to consent to or to support evil in any way. The Lord will show us the time and the weak point of our enemy where we may apply the grace of God.

The Lord can neutralize the problem in our heart, and whether or not the other person is saved depends on their attitude. It is sad that so many of those who plant evil start, or continue, a chain reaction that drags many others down.

In many parts of Colombia, it is common practice for people to kill or to have their enemies killed. The more subtle work of the Devil is to manage to kill, in our hearts, those who ought to be our friends. If he accomplishes this so that we no longer have a heart for our brothers and sisters in the faith, then he has his foot in the door, and he is going to work harder and harder to open the breach. What begin as feelings will sooner or later become converted into words and actions.

Scripture implies it is not even wise to bring railing accusations against the Devil (Jude 9). When facing the Devil over the body of Moses, the archangel Michael only said, "The Lord reprehend you." This was enough.

If our tongue is not under control and we continue to belittle others, this is a sure sign that our heart is not perfect. According to Scripture, out of the abundance of the heart the mouth speaks (Matthew 12:34).

The Lord has created us in such a manner that when there is a lot of emotion and we are under a lot of pressure, our mind disconnects, and what is in our heart comes straight out of our mouth.

When things are calm, when no one is putting any pressure on us and when nothing serious has happened, our mind can filter what is flowing out of our heart. It is when we are caught off guard that everyone finds out what was really in our heart because it comes pouring out of our mouth.

Times like this will even show us what is in our own heart. There are times when this can be beneficial because there are situations when it is important to say what we really feel and think. There are moments when we must speak the truth and confront someone.

Stephen did this and it cost him his life (Acts 7). This type of thing has cost many people their lives because the Word is a double-edged sword.

What does the Lord desire? That we be upright in heart. When he has us upright in heart, he wants to keep us upright in heart.

For if our heart is right with God, and the Lord reigns in our heart, then when there is trouble and we are squeezed, what comes out of our heart is from God. Sometimes the Word of God cuts very deep, but it will be without malice.

11 *Be glad in the LORD and rejoice, ye righteous, and shout for joy, all ye that are upright in heart.*

## Let us pray:

*Heavenly Father, we ask that we might be able to learn from the experiences of others, beginning with the experience of David. We ask that we might yield our hearts to your commands. We ask that we may desire to keep our hearts pure and clean, so we might be among the upright in heart who rejoice and shout for joy.*

*We ask this in the name of our Lord Jesus,*

*Amen.*

# Healings in Colombia

*By Alethia Stendal*

Albert's visit to Colombia in January of 2014 came as a breath of fresh air. He had written saying he was scheduled to fly in on January 13th and stay until the 26th. I asked him if he could extend his trip a week, and even though he had to pay an extra 300-dollar penalty, he did. I told him his money was well spent, and he wouldn't regret it. Then I received an email from him saying he felt too tired and stressed out, and he thought it would be better if he stayed home and came another time. Although I was a little disappointed, I told him to do whatever gave him peace. After about a week, he wrote back and said, "You know, I realized that for the past year whenever I was headed to Cuba and Colombia, the Devil attacked me before I left. I think this is another one of those attacks, and I have decided to come."

We met at the airport on the morning of January 13th and flew to Neiva, a city in the southern part of the country. Doctor Hugo Tovar Marroquín, the distinguished lawyer who was President Uribe's friend, picked us up from the airport and invited us to his house for breakfast. On the drive, Doctor Hugo received a text saying his mother had died. After twenty long minutes of uncertainty, he received another call from someone saying it had been someone else's mother who died. I thought it might be a good time to ask him if he wanted Albert to pray for his mother. After thinking she was dead a few minutes ago, of course he was enthused about it, and we went to her house.

First, Albert prayed for him and he was healed from a persistent back problem. His mom, the cutest little old lady, was waiting for us when we got to her house. Everything that could be wrong with her was. Albert started with her arms. She couldn't move them anymore because the area beneath the two shoulders had caved in and formed two holes. Albert prayed and the caved-in areas were restored to normal!

With a twinkle in her eyes, she moved her arms up and down with no pain. Her heart and her lungs weren't functioning well because she had smoked when she was young. Due to an accident, she couldn't move one of her fingers anymore. This inhibited her from sewing, her favorite hobby. Albert prayed for her in the name of Jesus and her finger was restored, and she began to breathe better immediately. She had needed an oxygen mask before that. Little did we know that this little old lady would later be the key to the whole family and their friends. She had eight children, and it was obvious that all of them respected her because one by one they flooded my cell phone with calls to thank us because "mom was very happy." Now they all wanted to be prayed for. Doctor Hugo told me that whenever we had a chance, he would pay for our tickets to come back and pray for the rest of his family.

We continued farther south where we had other friends waiting for us. In our first meeting in Garzón, Albert began praying but after five minutes, he looked at me and said, "There's no anointing. What should we do?"

He asked me to address the people. I said, "Although seeing miracles is very nice, and it can awaken much faith, it will never be His ultimate goal for us. When the Lord Jesus was here, what he longed for more than any miracles was for his disciples to know his Father. He wanted them to discover His love and be one with Him. There needs to be a complete surrender to God. What is the use of having your back healed if you don't know who He is? And when you let Him direct your life in every detail, the big picture will turn out as it should. I learned this while making a movie: All I had to do was make sure every detail was where it needed to be to the best of my ability, and the big picture came out the way it was supposed to."

Then Albert told some stories where God had a direct hand in his life, and he began to pray for the people once again. Many of them were healed of different things. Ernesto, my Jewish friend, said although he wasn't the one being prayed for because he was at the other end of the room talking to a friend, all of a sudden he felt a warmth come over his own spinal cord until it was completely restored. This happened while Albert was praying for someone else's back. His one arm was also shorter than the other, and it grew to the length of the longer one!

I invited Spencer, a Mormon friend of mine, to the meeting because he had back problems. Albert discovered the cause of Spencer's problems to be one leg shorter than the other. When Albert prayed, Spencer's legs where healed.

A few months earlier, Spencer's dad, a leader in the Mormon Church, went through a difficult heart surgery and almost died. Since he had diabetes, he hadn't recovered fully, and the doctors were considering another surgery. This was something that his dad and family did not want to go through. So Spencer told his dad about what God had done for him, and the next day, Spencer brought his dad to the house where we were staying.

At first Spencer's dad was skeptical and asked us a lot of questions like, "Who gave you the authority to heal people?"

And Albert humbly answered, "The Lord Jesus gave me the authority."

Then the Mormon turned and asked me in Spanish, "But how do I know that he is genuine?"

I said, "The Lord Jesus said that we shall know them by their fruit. Albert has been coming to Colombia for thirty years and has witnessed thousands of miracles here, but he has never used his gifts of healing for his own personal gain. Every trip has been paid for with his money, and he never asks people to give him anything in exchange. That is hard to find among people with God-given gifts."

After asking a few more questions, he asked Albert to please pray for his heart. Albert prayed that the metal left from the surgery would disappear and a full and complete healing would take place. This encounter opened the door to their whole family. That day we went to pray for their aunts and uncles, nieces, grandma, and friends. God gave the Mormon family a tremendous blessing.

The next day we drove for an hour and a half for a meeting at a small, humble farm near the town of La Plata, an area known for having endured much violence and war. But the people who were waiting for us had decided to put their trust in God. They stood their ground when everything was against them, and He saw them through. Being faithful listeners of our radio station, they were anxiously awaiting one of the preachers who spoke on it – Albert. They served us a delicious, abundant lunch, and then Albert and I took a nap to have strength for the meeting. After a quick, ten-minute snooze, we saw that people had gathered in the garden, and Albert began to pray for them one by one as I translated for him. Here is the report they sent me afterward:

*A very special greeting to everyone. May the Lord bless you all, and I continually thank you for coming to this distant mountain in Huila, bringing us the love of the Lord. We hope that the fullness of that love will germinate in every corner of our Colombia that you visit. May the Bright and Morning Star always guide your path.*

*Sonia, our neighbor, no longer suffers from the extreme pain she had in her hip every day.*

*Javier, a man who had a grave sickness that lowered his immunity, could never work because he would have a crisis. He started to work on his farm harvesting coffee and cutting grass the very next day without getting tired. His relatives are shocked and telling him to get examined, but his wife told them no because it is the work of the Lord and that made me happy. My daughter had been scheduled for a hip exam, and now she doesn't need it – thanks to the Lord.*

*I also had an uneven hip, and it hurt when I carried things. Now I can carry a heavy load and nothing hurts. I also feel very light when I walk. I give thanks and honor to the Lord every day for healing me through the hand of Albert and Alethia.*

*Kelly had a deviated bone in her spinal column that hurt every time she sat down, and now she is very thankful.*

*My friend Jimeno told me that he doesn't feel his hip is tired anymore, and he's been working in construction. He gives many thanks to the Lord and Albert.*

*David now feels no pain in his back, and he is content.*

*My son, Israel David, was also healed of his hip problem.*

*Aguilar suffered from an accident, and his arm would occasionally pop out of its socket. Now it doesn't.*

*Blessed be the name of the Lord because great and marvelous are all His works.*

*God bless Brother Albert and Alethia and all their friends for remembering the weakest. We love you and will always have you in our hearts.*

*Pabel.*

At our next meeting, a lady asked Albert to pray for her baby's digestive track. Being a good, former detective for the US Navy, Albert began to drill her to discover the reason behind her baby's health problem. After many questions, he finally asked her if she was breastfeeding the baby, and she said no.

"Why aren't you breastfeeding your baby?"

She smiled half embarrassed and said, "Sir, it's just that I only have one breast. The other one is too small."

"Do you want me to pray that the smaller breast would be restored to the same size as the other one?"

With a bashful smile, the lady nodded her head in approval. She put her hand over her nonexistent breast, and Albert put his hand on hers and prayed that it would grow to the same size as the other. I saw the empty space in the shirt begin to form a lump, and the two breasts became the same size. It was amazing. Then Albert asked her if this ran in the family, and she said that her mom had that same problem.

"Tell her to come here and let me pray for her," Albert said. The mother of the lady came shyly up next to her daughter. Quickly, the breast grew to the full size of the other one. "See," he told them, "it is important to pray that this family curse be broken because it is possible your baby daughter could inherit the same problem."

That night Doctor Hugo called asking if we could please pray for German, his twenty-nine-year-old nephew who was dying of cancer. The next morning we were on a plane to Bogotá to pray for him. We arrived at a small, two-bedroom apartment overlooking one of the main highways where German's dad was waiting for us with his sick son, his daughter, and two nurses. Before he prayed for German, Albert wanted the dad to see that the flesh responded to the name of Jesus. So he measured German's dad's legs, and one was shorter than the other one. In the name of Jesus, he prayed that the shorter one would grow to the same length as the other one. And it did. After praying for the daughter and two nurses, Albert felt it was time to pray for the cancer-stricken German. Albert laid his hand on German's belly and as he did this, strong anointing flowed from his hand.

Albert turned to me and said, "I got an anointing going here, and I can't let go until it stops."

After he prayed for the young man, he took the opportunity to tell the family and nurses about what God had done in his life. He told them about being in World War II – how one time he got shot in the back and became completely handicapped. The doctors said he would likely end up in a wheelchair the rest of his life, but his wife took him to a lady with the gift of healing. The woman sang to him and simply said, "In the name of Jesus, get up and walk." And from that moment on, Albert was healed both emotionally and physically. Not only that, but he also received the gift of healing.

After about twenty minutes of strong anointing, German fell into a deep sleep. When he woke up, he said he knew that God had a plan for his life and was using this illness to glorify Himself. I gave him a copy of *La Montaña*, and he immediately started watching it. The next day his dad called me and said his son was at the mall with his friends.

The rest of Hugo's extended family was so touched that they drove a seven-hour trip to Bogotá to have Albert pray for them. About ten of them arrived at the house. One of them was a lady who was talking loudly on her cell phone the whole time Albert was trying to pray for people, and he had to tell her to turn it off. When it came time for her turn, she asked for prayer for her eyes. Before I had time to ask her what was wrong with her eyes, Albert began to see a vision of them. He said, "The Lord has just revealed to me that you see spots everywhere." I asked her if this was the case and she said yes. So, knowing exactly how to pray for her, Albert prayed that she might have a normal vision with no spots, and she did.

One memorable miracle happened to a man who had chest pain and didn't know why. When Albert prayed for him, he saw in a vision that one of his lungs was obstructed. Again the Lord had showed Albert exactly how to pray. The man began to breathe and feel completely fine.

Another lady asked Albert to pray for her obesity and he said, "The only one who can do something about that is you." A lady with diabetes asked for prayer, and Albert explained the difference between alkaline and acid food and that people should eat more alkaline food than acid if they want to avoid diabetes. Another lady's muscles ached tremendously, and Albert told her that she had a magnesium deficiency, and she also needed more B6 and B12. This would help her muscles.

One of the things I learned is that although God can heal us, the Lord can't do our homework for us. We have to be conscious of the fact that God gave us a brain, and we should use our common sense and ask Him to show us how to be healthier. He may show you not to eat a certain thing because it is affecting your kidneys, and He may show me something completely different.

Although He can give us wisdom and discernment concerning our health, He does not intend for this to become an obsession to the point that we are completely focused on ourselves. He wants us to take the focus off ourselves and onto Him. Many people get side-tracked with diets and healthy precautions, saying, "I don't eat this," or, "I don't eat that." They say, "I just don't eat!" or, "The doctor said this or that," and what happens is their lives revolve around the wrong thing and they become powerless to be effective for God.

The next day we went to visit a woman who had four surgeries on her throat for cancer. When Albert prayed for her, she started sweating and said she was hot all over. Albert said that was the effect of the Holy Spirit working on her body. We conversed with her and her husband for a while until she said trivially, "I have anger issues that I am trying to resolve. I get upset at things easily, and I don't know how to control it."

Again, while using his detective skills, Albert said, "The mystery is solved! When you get angry, your stress goes up, and high stress lowers your immune system and leaves the door open for any disease to come in. That might be contributing to the cancer problem."

Albert explained how his father had rage problems, and it had passed on to his brother and eventually killed him at a young age. He said the only way to break this curse that we all inherit as a result of the fall of mankind is in the life of Jesus. When we live His life instead of our own, we become a new creation, and that is when all things become new – even an inherited anger problem. However, there is a price to pay – our life in exchange for His. Our plans become submitted to His plans, and our desires become His desires because of the work He is doing in our hearts. He is the only one who can break any bondage we have inherited.

The next day, we flew to another part of the country to pray for the Paez Indians. These fifty Christian families were displaced from their lands when a volcano destroyed everything, leaving them with nothing. The new land and homes provided by the government were given to the tribal leaders, who did not share with these families that refused to renounce their Christian beliefs and follow the tribal rituals. Years before, American missionaries had come to these areas. Decades later we are still seeing the fruit of what they planted. For seven years these Indians had to live in the most inhumane conditions, under garbage bags and with no running water or electricity. But they were patient and would not renounce their faith. The day came when God miraculously provided new land for them through the help of faithful brethren from Finland.

Alaskan electricians and professionals came to equip the new little Indian village with purified running water and electricity. Most of the children suffered from parasites and malnutrition. Doctor Fernando had already been there with medication for them. When Albert and I arrived, the children of the tribe wanted to play catch and other games with me. After a few hours of playing, it started getting dark. I took the littlest boy by the hand with me and headed to where Albert was waiting in the little, wooden, dirt-floor church they had built out of bamboo.

The rest of the thirty children followed close behind. Albert sat the little boy on a chair next to him, and sure enough, he had one leg a lot shorter than the other one. And it was healed in the name of Jesus. One by one, the rest of the children began coming up for prayer. Pretty soon moms with their babies started coming for prayer. There was so much anointing that most were healed of something. There is nothing that God can work with more than the heart of a child, and the place was full of children.

In another meeting in the city of Cali, Albert prayed for

a teenage boy who had a mental disorder and could not talk. When someone is unable to talk, Albert gets them to sing. We sang "Jesus Loves Me" to him, but the boy was not able to follow along. The next morning the boy's sister called, happy because her brother woke up singing!

I called Doctor Hugo and told him we had time to go back to the city of Neiva to pray for the rest of his relatives and friends. Little did we know that this lawyer seemed to know half the people in the city, and they all needed prayer. With the day completely full, we stayed for the night, and Don Hugo had to extend our plane ticket an extra day. He took Albert and me from house to house, praying for the rich and the poor. We went from visiting million-dollar mansions to the most humble neighborhoods. People's faith increased so much that they started bringing Albert their pets.

One family brought him a cat who had a broken leg and couldn't walk. When Albert prayed for the little kitty, the kitty immediately started to prance around the whole house. Five minutes before having to get to the airport we stopped at another house and a lady brought out a cage full of birds that needed prayer. Albert prayed for the little birds and we quickly left for the airport.

More people were waiting for us when we got there. Albert quickly prayed for them. I especially remember the face of a sweet old lady that Albert prayed for. I don't know what her sickness was, but I remember her face of pure gratitude as tears filled her eyes and she hugged us goodbye.

We went into the gate at the airport and found out our flight was delayed for forty minutes. I called the lawyer to tell him, and he talked to the security personnel. They opened the gate for us to pray for more people while we waited for our flight. The lawyer must have called more of his friends because more people came to the airport. By the time Albert got done praying for them, the airport security guards wanted prayer too! So Albert started praying for all of them one by one. Most of them had terrible back problems. Then the airport maids started coming for prayer. And before we knew it, the flight attendants of the airline were asking for prayer.

We seemed to have had time for a little revolution at the airport while we waited for our plane to arrive. We got back in our gate and prayed for a few more flight attendants and security people. Then finally we got on our flight back to Bogotá. I had never seen such a happy, little airport before.

A young guy picked us up from the airport and drove to my house. Everything in his body was hurting, and no matter how much Albert prayed for him, he didn't seem to improve. When he and his driver left our house, Albert and a friend from Alaska, named Jon Dufendach, both received discernment from the Lord. The Lord showed them that this guy wasn't healed because he was holding on to something dark in his life.

A few hours later, a blind lady arrived at our house. She had called to ask my dad to speak at her church, but instead my dad said, "How is your health?" She ended up taking a cab to where we were. Years before, she had had two tumors in her right eye, and the doctors said she needed surgery but would definitely lose her eye. When she was in the hospital, she didn't have peace about it, so she burst out of the operating room, escaped the hospital, and took a cab home.

The Lord led her to a hospital run by a Christian doctor. He told her, "Look, I will be honest with you because I don't know if you will like this. The truth is that I place God and His wisdom first. He comes before all the books I've ever learned from, and I am going to ask Him to give me wisdom as to how to treat you. I will do as He shows me. Is that okay with you?" Well, she was so happy. This was an answer to prayer. The Christian doctor operated on her and was able to remove the two tumors without having to eliminate her eye.

But days after her surgery, her eye became infected. For six months she had to endure this until the eye went completely dark like a black screen. The good eye was old and worn out so it didn't work well either. When she told us about her eyes, she said, "But my eyes come second. What I really want is for the Lord to restore my first love for Him, because I feel I've lost it."

Albert laid his hand on her eyes and began praying for her. When he stopped, she said, "Pray a little more, I can see 90 degrees out of it, but I need to be able to see 130." So he prayed more. Then he stopped and she said, "Okay, now I can see, but it's like looking through spider webs." Albert said that what she was seeing were her own veins. He prayed that the blood pressure in the veins would return to normal in the name of Jesus, and when he took his hand off and she opened both eyes, she began to weep. I have never seen anyone so delighted in a miracle healing before.

Crying she gasped, "My God, I can see! My God, thank you so much; I can see again. Marina, Alethia, I can see!" She called her husband and said, "Honey, the Lord restored my vision, I can see!" Her husband, an orthopedic surgeon, started weeping on the other end of the telephone line. It was one of the most amazing moments I have ever witnessed. She was overjoyed.

Albert said to her, "Now you don't need to question your first love anymore because you know that God loves you so much that He gave you back your eyes."

Then my dad took Albert to pray for General Barrero. And the Lord touched him too.

Russell Stendal, a former hostage of Colombian rebels, is a lifelong missionary to that same group in the jungles of Colombia. He is an influential friend to military and government leaders in Colombia, Cuba, Mexico, Venezuela, and the United States. Russell's ministry shares the gospel via twelve radio stations, hundreds of thousands of Bibles, books, and movies distributed through airplane parachute drops, and numerous speaking engagements for groups of leaders, prisoners, and individuals. Russell goes wherever the Lord leads, whether it's to speak with a president or to go deep into the jungle to help an individual in trouble. He has witnessed thousands commit their lives to Christ.

**Connect with Russell:** www.cpcsociety.ca

**Receive newsletter updates:** http://eepurl.com/qmazf

Alethia Stendal has been a photographer/ videographer in Colombia for the past ten years. She has written and directed several documentaries about the war in Colombia. She has also been involved in the production of audio material such as the MegaVoice English Bible and has co-edited several books in English including "The Book of Daniel" by her father, Russell Stendal. In recent years, Alethia, has been the co-writer/director/producer of the full-feature film La Montaña. She also did the wardrobe design for the film. Currently she lives in Bogota, Colombia with her husband, Stephen Miller, and travels extensively inside and out of the country promoting her film and increasing awareness on issues of the conflict in Colombia.

# Additional Stendal Titles

**ABOVE:** The ex-governor of Boyaca, Luis Humberto Montejo, and Alethia talking to two members of the FARC secretariat, Pablo Catatumbo and Ivan Márquez.

**BELOW:** Giving a Galcom radio with the recording of the Bible to Pablo Catatumbo.

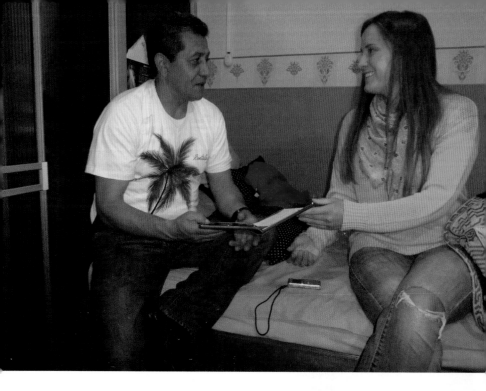

ABOVE & BELOW: Giving the movie signed by Noel to Jorge Pirata.

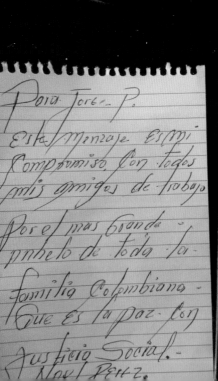

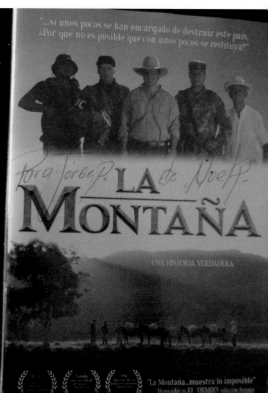

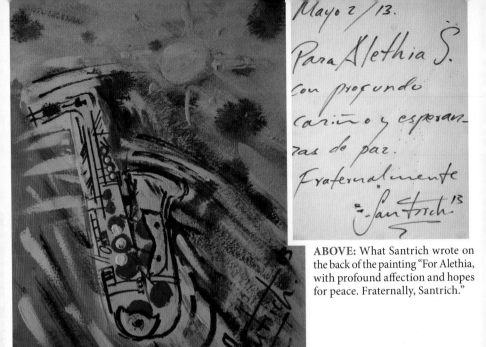

Mayo 2 / 13.

Para Alethia S.
con profundo
cariño y esperan-
zas de paz.
Fraternalmente
Santrich '13

**ABOVE:** What Santrich wrote on the back of the painting "For Alethia, with profound affection and hopes for peace. Fraternally, Santrich."

**LEFT:** Santrich gave Alethia this painting on her first trip to Cuba.

**BELOW:** This is the bike Luis Humberto and Russell Stendal designed especially for Santrich, who is blind.

**LEFT:** Alethia and Santrich.

**BELOW:** Lisa and Alethia in Cuba with their favorite real-life character, Noel.

**ABOVE:** Tom Howes and Russell Stendal signing each other's books.

**BELOW:** Tom Howes with Russell and Alethia.

**ABOVE & BELOW:** Alethia's encounters with President Uribe. The first time they met, he signed a copy of his book for her, "For Alethia, with admiration and gratitude. Alvaro Uribe Vélez."

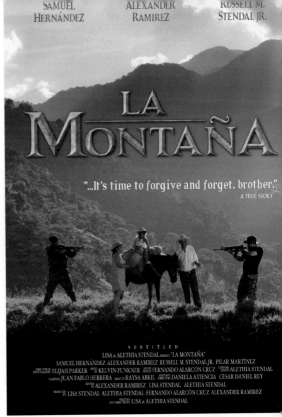

**BELOW:** Directing *La Montaña*. We had so many perfect moments like this, in which the picture had turned out exactly the way we had always imagined it. In the back are two of the main actors: Lisa's husband, Samuel Hernandez, who portrays Martin; and Russell Stendal Jr., who plays the paramilitary leader, Gabriel.

**ABOVE:** Dinner with Albert, Doctor Fernando and his wife Sol Beatrice, Russell and his wife Marina, and Alethia, in between Noel and Yuri.

**BELOW:** Russel with his wife, four children, son-in-law, mother-in-law (a Yuruti Indian), and two grandchildren.

**ABOVE:** Russell Stendal explaining Clayt Sonmore's book, *Master's of Deception*, to Ivan Márquez.

**BELOW:** The first encounter between Clayt Sonmore and Ivan Márquez.

**ABOVE:** Clayt Sonmore had an unforgettable encounter with Santrich.

**BELOW:** Russell Stendal, Ivan Marquéz, Clayt Sonmore, and Jesús Santrich after an extraordinary day.

**ABOVE:** *La Montaña* premier at the Colombian Army Base where we were given weapons, uniforms, security and extras to film it.

**BELOW:** Ivan Márquez, Russell Jr., Dylan, and Russell Sr. have a friendly talk as they overlook the ocean.

**ABOVE:** Noel, Yuri, Rodrigo Granda, Luis Humberto, and Russell Stendal.

**BELOW:** Noel with Russell Stendal, signing copies of *La Montaña*.

**ABOVE:** In La Picota prison with an ex-paramilitary man, who had received Russell Stendal's *Rescue the Captors* book years before on one of Russell Stendal's trips out to his area, and had kept it all these years for him to sign it. He was happy when he was finally able to get his signature.

**BELOW:** In prison with Jaime, the paramilitary ideologist. The prison is filled with colorful walls due to the work of his talented hands.

**ABOVE:** With General Barrero, a true leader and someone we will always admire.

**BELOW:** Russell Stendal with three of the top guerrilla leaders, Ivan Márquez, Jesús Santrich, and Rodrigo Granda.

**ABOVE:** Russell Stendal with Ivan, Pablo, Luis Humberto, Albert, David, and Yuri.

**BELOW:** The FARC celebrated their 50-year anniversary May 27, 2014. We also celebrated our 50-year anniversary in Colombia January 3, 2014.
Here is Luis Humberto and Russell Stendal among pictures of two of the main FARC leaders who are now deceased; Jacobo Arenas and Manuel Marulanda. These men ordered Russell Stendal's release from his kidnapping and promised Russell he could do missionary work in areas controlled by the FARC without being harmed. Manuel was known among his men for keeping his word. The picture between them is Simon Trinidad, another main leader, who is now serving a long sentence in a maximum security prison in Colorado.

**ABOVE:** This is the baby girl who was miraculously born after both Albert and Clayt prayed for her.

**BELOW:** Famous photo, "Change and Respect." (Photo by Steven Salisbury).